Also available at all good book stores

9781801500630

9781801500067

9781785319792

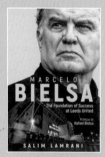

9781801501385

9781801500531

9781785319938

9781801501842

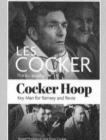

9781801501477

9781801501835

LEAGUE ONE
LEEDS

LEAGUE ONE
LEEDS

A JOURNEY THROUGH THE ABYSS

ROCCO DEAN

First published by Pitch Publishing, 2022

Pitch Publishing
9 Donnington Park,
85 Birdham Road,
Chichester,
West Sussex,
PO20 7AJ
www.pitchpublishing.co.uk
info@pitchpublishing.co.uk

ISBN 978 1 80150 399 0

Typesetting and origination by Pitch Publishing
Printed and bound in India by Replika Press Pvt. Ltd.

CONTENTS

FOREWORD

by Simon Grayson

League One Leeds is a detailed and passionate account of three seasons watching Leeds United in the third tier of English football. It was the lowest period in the club's history, but the author promotes the idea that football is about emotions, stories and experiences, and any Leeds fan who watched the club through this period will know that these three seasons provided all the thrills and spills that makes football what it is, even if it was at a level nobody associated with the club would want or expect to compete in.

After supporting and playing for Leeds United (only a few games, but I was there from the age of 14 through to 22) I was given the opportunity to manage this great club. It was something that I never thought I would achieve but something I dreamt about, and that dream came true just before Christmas 2008. After a whirlwind few days I was leading my Leeds United team out in front of nearly 35,000 at Elland Road, and against Leicester City, who I had joined from Leeds as a player. This was the start of an incredible part of my life where this book goes into great detail.

League One Leeds is an informative and entertaining read for all Leeds supporters. It is well researched and the author's passion and knowledge shines through, bringing the feelings back to life all these years later. Yes, we hope the club never returns to League One, but the story of our time in the division will always remain a significant part of Leeds United's history.

PROLOGUE

Hero to Zero

Once upon a time I truly believed my presence at matches helped Leeds United win. When I started supporting Leeds they had seemingly blown their chance to become the last champions of the old First Division, but my three appearances between February and the end of the 1991/92 season yielded ten goals and nine valuable points for Howard Wilkinson's team as they stormed to an unlikely title. I'd done my bit; the players did the rest.

In the following season I had my first season ticket, on the front row of the West Stand directly behind the Leeds dugout, bang on the halfway line; 'the best seats in the house', as my dad would say on repeat. By December I still had a near-perfect record at Elland Road: eight wins, 30 goals scored, and three draws courtesy of late Leeds equalisers, making them even more exhilarating than the victories. A 4-1 defeat to Brian Clough's Nottingham Forest – on 'Old Big 'Ead's' last visit to Elland Road – was a shock to the system, but it was my only taste of defeat all season despite the reigning champions finishing 17th in the inaugural Premier League.

Gradually, my invincibility started to slip. There were two home defeats the following season and three the next; even so, with only six defeats from my first 66 trips to Elland Road I still felt like a good luck charm – only perennial champions Manchester United had a better home record than bang-average Leeds. By the time season 2007/08 rolled around I felt like a curse. Whenever it really mattered, Leeds lost.

Whenever they reached the threshold of glory, Leeds fell apart. The 21st century, in particular, had been an unmitigated disaster. Defeat in the Champions League semi-final, financial ruin, relegation from the Premier League, defeat in the play-off final, more financial ruin and another relegation, all in the space of six years.

The timing of the demise couldn't have been worse either. The Premier League was the place to be when Leeds were relegated from it, with sky-rocketing TV revenue making it the richest and most popular league in the world. It was fast becoming the strongest too, with Chelsea shooting to power thanks to the vast wealth of their new Russian owner, Roman Abramovich, who had just bought the debt-ridden club for £80m from Ken Bates. Abramovich wasn't the first foreign owner of a Premier League football club, but he was one of the first, and certainly the first who had enough money to blow the competition out of the water. The Russian oligarch laid the first stone of a very ugly road. Football clubs were clubs before the Premier League began; by the turn of the century they had become businesses, and through the 2000s they would become rich men's playthings, with Manchester City about to raise the bar again by introducing geopolitics into the mix with their Abu Dhabi takeover. Meanwhile, one of England's biggest clubs had shot their bolt a couple of years early and, crippled by debts of £100m with no oligarch waiting in the wings to save them, Leeds United fell into the abyss.

A part of me was excited when Leeds lost their Premier League status in 2004. Life in the newly branded Coca-Cola Championship would offer the chance to visit some new grounds and renew some old rivalries, and I fully expected Leeds to blow the opposition away. What goes down must come up, right? Not quite. Relegation wasn't all it was cracked up to be, and the Championship collectively laughed as they waved us on our merry way, down to League One.

Leeds United would now embark upon a journey which would take them to places they had never imagined and last longer than they ever feared. League One was a whole new ball game, but 'League One Leeds' followed everything we had come to expect from a soap opera of a football club: heartbreak, humiliation and a host of off-field dramas just to make sure football was never the only thing Leeds fans had to worry about.

PART ONE: 2007/08

US AGAINST THE WORLD

INTRODUCTION

By Jermaine Beckford

Summer 2007 was a bizarre time in my career. Leeds United had just been relegated from the Championship to League One, but I was getting promoted from League One to the Championship while on loan at Scunthorpe United. Dennis Wise was the gaffer at Leeds, with Gus Poyet his number two, and earlier in the season they sat me down in their office and told me they wanted to build the following season's team around me and my strengths, but in the meantime would be sending me out on loan to get more experience, and to get me away from all the carnage that was about to ensue. There were a lot of players the club needed to get off the books so they could start the re-building process at Elland Road, and they knew it wasn't going to be pretty. The atmosphere would turn quite toxic but they were thinking of the bigger picture.

Amid the excitement of working our way to automatic promotion at Scunthorpe, I was watching Leeds every single week hoping everything would be fine. It was the complete contrast and ended in relegation and administration. Although the situation was far from ideal, relegation and financial instability was never going to stop me going back to Leeds, I was going back there no matter what. If Leeds United had ended up playing non-league football I'd have still gone back, because it's a ridiculous, amazing football club.

Returning to training at Thorp Arch, I was completely confident that we had more than enough to deal with the coming season. Scunthorpe had great ethos, great ethics, and a team full of confidence, but, no disrespect to them, they didn't have the same quality individuals that we had at Leeds, so I knew for a fact we would have a successful season. As players, we knew what we were capable of and set our own targets. We planned to win a certain amount of games that would leave us on X amount of points, which would either get us promotion or into the play-offs, not a problem. What we didn't foresee was the 15-point deduction, but that just galvanised the squad that little bit more. It gave us the siege mentality, that 'us against the world' mindset.

Union Berlin 2 Leeds United 0
Pre-season friendly
Alte Forsterei (7,602)

> *'The players really wanted to play for Leeds United. It wasn't about the money because the money wasn't great, they just wanted to play for Leeds.' – Casper Ankergren*

Leeds United entered the third tier of English football with Ken Bates as owner, Dennis Wise as manager and Shaun Harvey as CEO. If that's not rock bottom just shoot me now! I never thought I'd live to see my beloved club relegated from the Championship, but the pain of relegation was overshadowed by a much darker reality, the uncertainty surrounding the club's very existence. With unserviceable debts totalling £35m, Bates had put United into administration and the whole summer was dominated by legal wrangling.

The potential saving grace of Leeds's on-field humiliation was the opportunity to start afresh, with no debt and an owner who had the club's best interests at heart. There were five consortiums competing to take control – one of which was led by Duncan Revie, the son of the great Don Revie, who had put Leeds United on the map. I was excited by the prospect of the club being back in the hands of a Revie again; instead, the very people responsible for putting Leeds in this mess regained control by the slenderest of margins. The winning bid required 75 per cent backing to succeed and, after a recount, the Bates regime prevailed with 75.2 per cent of the creditors' vote, this despite offering just a penny in the pound to the creditors. Bates's offer was significantly less than the competitors, but was the best offer overall thanks to Astor Investment Holdings mysteriously agreeing to waive their £17m debt if Bates was given the club. There was a 28-day cooling-off period for any unhappy creditors to lodge appeals, but possession is nine-tenths of the law and Bates had the keys to Elland Road so continued to run the club as best he could (theoretically).

It would be fair to say the supporters didn't take kindly to the news that the hierarchy who took Leeds to the lowest point in their history were back at the helm, and Bates was already unpopular with the fans long before he got his hands on their club. Being ex-Chelsea was a bad start, his outspoken nature and dodgy dealings were a nuisance, but historic declarations of war on Leeds United were unforgivable in the eyes of many, even two decades on from when the following quote emerged, 'I shall not rest until Leeds United are kicked out of the Football League. Their fans are the scum of the earth, absolute animals and a disgrace. I will do everything in my power to make sure this happens.'

Irrespective of his past, I saw Bates as a shrewd businessman who was capable of leading the club out of League One, but the fact he had led us there in the first place was enough for me to always join in fervently with regular chants of 'GET THE CHELSEA OUT OF LEEDS!' Those chants were water off a duck's back to old 'Cuddly Ken', who wasn't shy in giving it back to the supporters either, 'Dennis, Gus and myself are here for the long haul. So the mindless minority who do their silly chants had better get used to it.' It was a sentiment reflected by the manager, who would not shy away from his unpopularity either, 'The supporters don't like Batesy and they don't particularly like me, but they've got us. It's time to march on and stick together.'

Their comments were a little premature. On 3 July, just an hour before the 3pm deadline for creditor appeals, HMRC – who were due to receive only £77,000 from a £7.7m debt – lodged an appeal against the awarding of the club to Bates, this despite Bates increasing his offer to 8p in the pound to stave off any legal challenge (thus increasing the payment due to HMRC to £616,000). It wasn't so much the offer they were unhappy with, but the technical grounds on which the club was sold back to Bates. On 6 July, with the hearing for HMRC's appeal set for 3 September, the administrators had no choice but to put Leeds United back up for sale. They didn't have the funds to run the club for two months in lieu of a new owner, and even if they did, the Football League were unlikely to permit Leeds to start the season in administration. With just three days to prepare bids with proof of funding, there was only one competitor for Bates, so this time there was no surprise that the club was once again sold to his newly formed company, Leeds United Football Club Limited. Bates paid £1.5m for the club, with the creditors now receiving 11.2p in the pound (with the exception of Astor Investment, whose £17m was duly written off).

Jermaine Beckford: 'I fully understand how Ken Bates rubbed people up the wrong way. From a fan's perspective – someone who appreciates and cares for the club like it's their own – you can't help but look at the administration situation and think, "How on earth has he been able to do this and get away with it?" But successful people have to do certain things to get their own way, especially if it's something they truly believe in. And it was for the greater good. The club was going down the pan, it was inevitable they would have ended up in financial ruin.'

That wasn't the end of it though; it was just the start. Because of HMRC's legal challenge, Leeds were unable to exit administration with a CVA (a statement confirming the majority of creditors agreed to the sale) as required by Football League rules. Instead, the administrators had made a direct sale to Bates, and without a CVA the Football League refused to grant Leeds their 'golden share' to compete in the 2007/08 season. Amid the uncertainty, season ticket holders received a letter from Bates explaining that season ticket money would be refunded if Leeds couldn't start the season. If the letter was supposed to be reassuring it had the opposite effect on me; I found it absolutely galling. A £400 refund would be scant consolation for having no football club to support.

Due to the administration palaver Leeds had no competition to prepare for, they were operating under a transfer embargo, and they hadn't paid their players for six weeks.

Jonny Howson: 'Yeah, I managed all right for money. I was still living at home with my mum and dad, and they didn't charge me rent or board or anything like that, so I was fortunate. But you are aware that other people's careers and livelihoods were on the line. As much it didn't affect me, I had the passion and love, and grew up supporting Leeds, but of course there were others who thought, "I'm not sticking around for this."'

The club soldiered on with their pre-season plans regardless, and a 20-man squad headed to Germany on a tour. Frazer Richardson, Jonathan Douglas, Seb Carole, Ian Westlake, Trésor Kandol and Jermaine Beckford were the retained first-teamers, with Jonny Howson, Ben Parker, Fabian Delph, Tom Elliot and Rob Bayly brought along from the youth team. Alan Thompson, Matt Heath, Rui Marques and Tore André Flo were hoping to earn new contracts once the transfer embargo was lifted, and they were joined by five trialists who weren't just making up the numbers. Among them was David Prutton, a 27-year-old midfielder who had played over 200 games for Nottingham Forest and Southampton, with over 60 of those coming in the Premier League. Another was Leon Constantine, who was hot property having scored 22 goals in League One for Port Vale the previous season. It was indicative of what a huge pull Leeds United were at this level, that this calibre of player would join for pre-season with no guarantee of a contract and plenty of other options on the table, and it was heartwarming to know how much the squad that travelled to Germany really wanted to play for Leeds.

> *David Prutton: 'As soon as I knew Leeds was an option I didn't really want to go anywhere else. There was an element of risk, but as a group we trusted that Dennis would put a contract in front of us as soon as he could, and presumed Ken Bates would sort out the administration side. Plus, when you're young and in your 20s you don't really worry about all that! "Leeds United want me to go and play for them? Yes please! I'm there with bells on, give me the white shirt!"'*

My friends Paul, Rick, Gaz and I also made the trip to Berlin. We spent three days in the historic German capital and had a great time. We didn't take in any culture, did no sight-seeing and took no photos, we simply drank all day in the blazing sun while playing four-way poker (using Tic-Tacs as chips), then drank all night. The match with Union Berlin was the only break in the cycle, although the early evening kick-off meant we could still drink all day in the blazing sun, but instead of playing poker we chatted and chanted with the rest of the Leeds fans before heading to the ground. The game itself is a blur (surprise, surprise), but I remember being stood on a decrepit terrace behind the goal with no roof to shade us from the still-blazing sun, and being impressed by the atmosphere in a small and unloved stadium. Less impressive were Leeds, who played like the bunch of strangers they practically were.

After a 2-0 defeat we were back in Berlin replenishing our alcohol levels when we realised Dennis Wise and his coaching staff were sitting at the table next to us, on the other side of some shrubbery. We began discussing how much we hated our manager in obnoxiously loud voices, resulting in Wise's assistant, Gus Poyet, coming over and pleading with us to have more respect for the man who had dragged our play-off finalists down to League One. Sadly, the German lager robbed me of any further memories of the altercation, although I do remember chatting in the bar with Alan Thompson, who was singing Wise's praises and adamant he would lead us back to the Championship. The positive feeling towards the management team was unanimous throughout the squad.

Jemaine Beckford: 'Dennis and Gus were a great double act. From the outside looking in you would think Gus was the nice guy and Wise was the beast, but it wasn't like that, they could each be the good cop or the bad cop. They bounced off each other really well.'

It had been an unprecedentedly turbulent summer, but at 6.30pm on Friday, 3 August, just one week before the season began, Leeds were finally granted their golden share, securing their place in League One. However, it came at an unprecedented cost: they would begin the new season on minus 15 points. It was the heaviest points deduction ever handed out by the Football League, who explained that with no creditor-backed CVA, Ken Bates had effectively wiped out the club's debts just by calling in the administrators, an act that could not go unpunished. Bates immediately appealed against the points deduction, but two days before the season started the sanction was confirmed following a vote by the chairmen of the other Football League clubs. As Bates had signed an agreement that no legal action could be taken against the Football League the matter was considered closed, but he would not take the decision lying down and appealed to the FA for their intervention. Bates labelled the ruling 'an unlawful miscarriage of justice' and believed the issue should have been handled by an independent tribunal, not by 69 self-interested competitors.

'They've already cut off my arms and legs, now they've cut my balls off as well,' was the famous quote from Wise, and with only five clubs voting in Leeds's favour a siege mentality was created within Elland Road. 'Us against the world' had been at the heart of Leeds's mantra since the club was founded out of the ashes of Leeds City, who were expelled from the Football League for fielding ineligible players during the First World War, a practice that was understood to be common throughout the league. Fast forward 88 years, and under similarly shady circumstances the club had at least managed to retain their place in the Football League and keep their name (except for the 'A' from 'Leeds United AFC', and I really liked that letter). Finding solace in these two minimum requirements was really scraping the bottom of the barrel, and Ray Fell, chairman of the Leeds United Supporters' Club, summarised the feelings of the fanbase, 'The fans are bewildered by it all. It is a recipe for relegation.'

The fear of relegation was backed up by the past, the present, and the predictors of the future. In the history of English football only six teams had received points deductions and they had all been relegated at the end of the season. History only dictates so much, but in the here and now Wise's team had lost six of their last seven pre-season friendlies, and the bookies – so often correct – slashed the odds for Leeds being relegated to League Two. I braced myself for the worst as Leeds jumped into the abyss.

———

Tranmere Rovers 1 Leeds United 2

Matchday 1 of 46
Prenton Park (11,008)

> *'Minus 15 made the squad stronger. You had nothing to lose. Typical Dennis Wise, us against them, that's his character.' –*
> *Casper Ankergren*

The new season was finally upon us and Leeds were alive and kicking, 24th in League One and 15 points adrift without kicking a ball. Despite having only eight days to sign players, by kick-off at Tranmere Wise had scrambled a squad together and believed he had a 'group' that was strong enough to overcome their 15-point deficit and achieve promotion.

Without the weight of a £35m debt around his neck, Bates was feeling flush and sanctioned a £500,000 spending spree once the transfer embargo was lifted. 'Don't spend it all at once,' he might have said, but within 24 hours Wise had spent the lot on nine players. The majority went on Norwich City's versatile midfielder Andy Hughes, the trialists and out-of-contract players were rewarded with the deals they were promised, and the remaining funds were spent bringing Casper Ankergren back from Brøndby. The Danish goalkeeper had spent the second half of the previous season on loan at Elland Road, and his recollections of summer 2007 portray the instability that was forced upon the players, although in Casper's case it was self-inflicted.

> *Casper Ankergren: 'Dennis Wise really wanted to keep me, but I still had a contract with Brøndby who wanted to sell me to a Norwegian club. I completely shut that down. I really wanted to go back to Leeds because I felt the passion the people had for football, even if that meant waiting until the end of the transfer window. It was only four days before the season started that I finally signed. I hadn't played, or even had a proper pre-season, but I was straight in at Tranmere.'*

One signing who wouldn't be making his debut at Tranmere was Leon Constantine. An ankle injury in the final pre-season match robbed Dennis Wise of his new striker for the first three months of 2007/08, so Leeds would start with a duo who had only played together once for the club. Physically they looked like they could be a decent partnership – Trésor Kandol was big and Jermaine Beckford was fast – but both were as raw as it comes. Kandol was 25 and had only scored a dozen professional-level goals, while Beckford was 23 and had only played half a season in professional football.

> *Jermaine Beckford: 'My loan at Scunthorpe did wonders for me. I was playing games, scoring goals, winning games, and getting an understanding of what it takes to be a professional footballer. It reinforced my belief that I was good enough, that I was capable, that I could make it in the game.'*

A historic afternoon for Leeds United was a landmark occasion for right-back Frazer Richardson, who would make his 100th appearance for the club at Prenton Park. Richardson was one of a teamful of graduates that came through the fruitful Thorp Arch academy around the turn of the century, and if fate hadn't transpired so badly Leeds could have been opening the 2007/08 season with a team of homegrown players who were in, or approaching, their prime: Paul Robinson, Frazer Richardson, Ian Harte, Jonathan Woodgate, Matt Kilgallon, Matthew Jones, Stephen McPhail, James Milner, Aaron Lennon, Alan Smith and, well, Scott Carson I suppose. Instead, the historic starting 11 was: Casper Ankergren, Frazer Richardson, Eddie Lewis, Rui Marques, Matt Heath, Andy Hughes, Alan Thompson, Curtis Weston, Ian Westlake, Jermaine Beckford and Trésor Kandol.

I was 23 years old and still living at home, and working for my dad's flood restoration business, Chem-Dry of Harrogate, who were dealing with the worst flooding (or best, in our eyes) to hit the UK since records began. In non-flood times we would have 30 to 40 ongoing jobs, but now we were dealing with 1,300; a challenge of epic proportions. The handful of trained staff we had weren't allowed any time off – we worked around the clock for seven days a week, and even holidays were cancelled – so, instead of being in the ground for the opening day of the League One season, I was driving back to Yorkshire from Surrey.

Leeds United playing their first ever game in England's third tier was big news, and I was pleased to be receiving regular updates from talkSPORT while racing against time to get back into Radio Leeds bandwidth and catch what I could of the full match commentary. I was less pleased when what might have been a regular, halfway-through-the-half update, gleefully revealed that Leeds had fallen behind. At least it was a Leeds fan who scored the first goal of the League One era, and Tranmere's Chris Greenacre couldn't resist giving a quick 'Leeds salute' to the travelling fans behind the goal. It was a fittingly bizarre way to open what was fast becoming the most bizarre season in the club's history. talkSPORT's half-time report suggested the visitors were lucky to only be a goal behind, but the Whites came out fighting after the break and deservedly levelled through Matt Heath.

It was pedal to the metal up the M1. With a vanful of dehumidifiers it was difficult to exceed the speed limit, but I gave it everything I could. Meadowhall is a significant milestone on the journey up the M1 as it confirms entry back into Yorkshire, and at this point the struggle to receive Radio Leeds commenced. As the game headed into its final minutes I was still failing to get reception, so it was through talkSPORT that I learned of a dramatic last-gasp winner in the big game in League One. It had gone to Leeds, with Kandol somehow bundling a cross from Andy Hughes through the goalkeeper's legs and into the net. I was ecstatic; what a way to start the season!

Thereafter I managed to tune in to Radio Leeds and rejoice in all the post-game reaction, with everyone seemingly stunned at what they had witnessed. Even more stunning than the lucky late winner was Kandol's subsequent cartwheel (quite an achievement for a man of his size and elegance) but most stunning of all was the transformation in team spirit for the second half. The lads had pulled together like a proper team, not just a bunch of players thrown together in the final days of pre-season. Dennis Wise had clearly instilled an 'us against the world' attitude, although he was hardly selling rain to the Mancunians – considering the goings-on of the summer it was impossible for the squad to feel any different.

After saluting the Leeds fans at the final whistle, the players, led by Wise, formed a big celebratory huddle in the middle of the pitch. 'You can't pre-plan celebrations like that after the game,' said Wise. 'That was natural. That shows how close the group is.' The Whites were up and running, and according to their manager it was a case of three points down, just another 102 to go.

——

Leeds United 4 Southend United 1

Matchday 2 of 46
Elland Road (24,005)

> *'Playing for Leeds United, there's pressure every single second! But the biggest pressure came from ourselves because we knew what we were capable of.' – Jermaine Beckford*

'Welcome back,' wrote Ken Bates proudly in his first programme notes of the season. 'Yes, we are still here despite the best efforts of opportunists, politicians and certain people who acted simply from motive of malice.' Bates was on the charm offensive, explaining that the club had been restructured to be 'leaner and meaner', and talking up the investments made to improve the matchday experience for the fans.

Howard's Way was a new bar, named in honour of Howard Wilkinson, 'The Father of Modern Leeds', and Bates had installed new corporate facilities too, the Legends Lounge in the South Stand, the Lorimer Suite in the East Stand, and the Bremner Suite in the West Stand. For all Bates spoke of improvements to the matchday experience, the only difference to me was the lack of a scoreboard. The big screen had gone kaput and the club couldn't afford to replace it until the following year (in the end, it wasn't replaced for two years). In terms of football, good news was so scarce that Ken's highlight of the summer had been the under-tens reaching 'the final of their section' in a junior tournament for local sides in southern France.

Despite all the close-season shenanigans, or because of them, it was a wonderful feeling to be taking my place at the back of section N11 in the Kop, standing alongside my best friend Paul who had a season ticket with me. We never sat in our actual seats though, we would just congregate on the stairs with our other friends, Rick, Joe and Corbett, and so many others that it resembled old-fashioned terracing, without the crush barriers to stop you tumbling all the way down the stairs in those rare moments of unbridled joy, otherwise known as the 'Elland Road Shuffle'.

Congregating on the stairs led to perpetual battles with the stewards. They had long since abandoned their quest to make everyone in the Kop sit down, but their new challenge was to keep the gangways clear. Once or twice a half, the stewards would make their way up the Kop stairs and the dozen or so in the Gangway Gang would shimmy into the seating, making everyone who was occupying their actual seats squeeze right in, before dispersing once the stewards left. Most of the time it was a source of amusement but sometimes a 'jobsworth' steward would try to check your tickets, and if tensions on the terraces were already raised by the action on the pitch, this would form a toxic concoction.

Leeds United's first home game in League One was also my nephew Louis's first ever game, sitting in the Family Stand with my dad and brother-in-law. Having been born a month after Leeds lost to Valencia in the 2001 Champions League semi-final, who would have thought Louis's first match at Elland Road would be in the third tier? It was a dream start for Louis, with Alan Thompson whipping a trademark 30-yard free kick into the top corner after just three minutes, and he would see a dream ending too.

A 70th-minute Southend equaliser could have punctured the atmosphere, but the 24,000 hardcore Leeds fans urged their team on and Tore André Flo's acrobatic 86th-minute goal brought the first Elland Road Shuffle of the season. In injury time, fan favourite Rui Marquez's near-post flick looped inside the far upright to seal the win, and being his first goal for Leeds added gloss to the celebrations. And there was still time for Jermaine Beckford to score his first goal for the club too, a clinical left-footed finish from the edge of the box. At full time, the players and staff once again formed a big huddle in the centre circle and the fans were in fine voice, 'NINE MORE POINTS TO GO, BEFORE WE GET TO ZERO!'

> *Jonny Howson: 'With the minus 15 there was a real togetherness through the whole club; the fans, the players and the staff. That was created by Dennis and Gus, they brought a real determination to the group and that's why we made such a good start. It was us against the world.'*

With three goals in the last five minutes it had been an exhilarating finish, and the fact that it had come in a League One match was irrelevant to everyone in attendance, especially Louis. It made me wonder what difference being in League One really made. When comparing Louis's first taste of Elland Road to my own there probably wasn't much difference, except in the quality of football. Leeds were fighting Manchester United to be champions of England when I attended my first game, but a 2-0 victory over Luton Town in front of 28,000 or a 4-1 win against Southend United in front of 24,000 was much of a muchness; when you boil it right down, it's just the Whites versus the visitors. As far as I could tell, the main drawback of being in League One was having to sit through *Match of the Day* and all the action from the Championship on *The Football League Show* before the Leeds highlights finally came on.

The following week came a clash of the division's titans – two former European Cup finalists – and Leeds prevailed 2-1 at Nottingham Forest thanks to another late goal, with Beckford diverting home in the 90th minute. The 100 per cent record continued as Beckford and Kandol's blossoming partnership carved out the only goal against Luton Town, who were managed by the man Dennis Wise had replaced in the Elland Road hotseat, Kevin Blackwell. The real drama came after the final whistle, when a roar went up from the West Stand as Wise and Blackwell engaged in some argy-bargy. 'He didn't want to shake my hand, unfortunately,' said Wise afterwards. 'I asked if he had a problem and he kindly told me to "something off". He was obviously upset he lost. It was probably the biggest game of his career and was very important to him.' The melee made waiting up until 1am to see the highlights worthwhile.

——

Leeds United 2 Hartlepool United 0
Matchday 5 of 46
Elland Road (26,877)

> *'My best goal? I don't know, there's a few to choose from! I quite liked that Hartlepool goal, technically that's definitely up there.' – Jermaine Beckford*

It had been a sensational opening month of the season for Leeds, better than anybody could have anticipated. They had seen off all comers on the pitch, and on the last day of August Ken Bates saw off HMRC, who dropped their challenge against the administrators' decision just three days before the hearing was due to take place. It was a slightly bittersweet conclusion – had they not challenged in the first place there would have been no 15-point deduction – but the administration saga was finally over and Bates had his clean slate, a debt-free Leeds United.

Bates was still expecting to have the points deduction overturned too, but he was still awaiting a response from the Football Association following his request for their intervention. 'This matter will not go away,' promised the chairman, one promise he was sure to keep. Yet behind Bates's outrage, you got the feeling he was revelling in this battle, and the Leeds supporters, so used to being unjustly downtrodden, were revelling in it too. Confidence was sky high, and promotion would taste all the sweeter off the back of such a harsh points deduction, a feeling that was reflected in a bullish new chant from the terraces, 'FIFTEEN POINTS, WHO GIVES A FUCK? WE'RE SUPER LEEDS AND WE'RE GOING UP!'

When Hartlepool United arrived in West Yorkshire, Leeds had the chance to wipe out their points deduction without the help of any men in suits (except Wise and Poyet, I suppose). It was the last hot day of the year and Elland Road was expecting nothing less than the victory that would take their side to zero points at the earliest possible opportunity. Despite the perfect start to the season Leeds's performances had been far from spectacular, but with a solid defence, a well-balanced midfield and a potent strike force, it was no wonder they were churning out wins. Beckford and Kandol were proving unstoppable for League One defences, and despite an unconvincing display, they grabbed a goal each to earn a 2-0 victory, with Beckford's exquisite touch and chip over the keeper (both with his weaker left foot) screaming, 'I'm the star of this team!'

Beckford had been at the club for 18 months without making any impact, and although a successful loan spell at Scunthorpe had suggested he could do a job at this level, few could have expected the ex-Wealdstone striker and RAC recovery man to show such scintillating form. Except perhaps, the player himself, and his manager.

Jermaine Beckford: 'Knowing your manager supports you 100 per cent does wonders for any player, especially a striker. I was going into games feeling confident, excited and happy.'

Beckford had all the attributes to be a top striker. He was as fast as lightning and a natural finisher, a fox in the box and capable of the spectacular outside of it. Coupled with his late arrival in professional football, comparisons were being made with the Arsenal legend Ian Wright, and Beckford's goal against Hartlepool would have graced any Wright highlight reel, which is no mean feat.

The post-match huddle had now become a trademark, and as the players and staff bounced around joyously a chant reverberated around Elland Road that had never been heard before and would surely never be heard again, 'ZERO! ZERO! ZERO!' For the first time since 'O'Leary's Babies' tore through Europe, there was a real feelgood factor at the club, and the manager who had been treated with disdain throughout his tenure was finally beginning to win over the fans. Dennis Wise must have wondered if he was hearing correctly when his name was chanted from the Kop, although the fans split the adulation between the boss and his assistant, the significantly more popular Gus Poyet. Despite my admiration for the job both ex-Chelsea men were doing, I still couldn't bring myself to join in.

Jonny Howson: 'As soon as you start doing well people will take to you, because you're giving your all for the club and you want to succeed. Wise was no different. When he first came in he upset a fair few while putting his own stamp on things, but it was different in League One because he had his own team.'

Beckford and Kandol continued their electric form by scoring all the goals in a midweek 3-0 victory at Bristol Rovers, with Beckford's brace again portraying his ability to find the net in whichever way was required. His first was a poacher's finish, and his second a spectacular overhead kick that sealed another flattering scoreline after Leeds had been forced to dig deep for most of the match. The three points lifted the Whites off the bottom of the table, and the following week they were out of the relegation zone with a 2-0 victory over Swansea at Elland Road. Seven wins out of seven had equalled the club's best ever start to a season, and the chants from the terraces were becoming more and more bullish by the week, 'WE'RE GOING UP AS FUCKING CHAMPIONS!'

Oldham Athletic 0 Leeds United 1

Matchday 9 of 46
Boundary Park (10,054)

'A combination of external factors spilled over in that moment. It was stupid, but when you're in the thick of it there's no reasoning with you. You want justice, you want what's right.' – Jermaine Beckford

Leeds were going about their business with little fuss on the pitch, but the off-field shenanigans continued unabated. Bates's appeal to the FA was dismissed, with English football's governing body deeming it inappropriate for them to investigate the Football League's processes. Bates appealed this decision too, and his CEO, Shaun Harvey, expressed the club's dismay, 'We are amazed the Football Association do not feel it is appropriate to intervene in a matter that we believe is fundamentally wrong, and sets a dangerous precedent for the future.'

It wasn't just the chairman who was on the warpath with the game's authorities; United's management team were at it too. Gus Poyet had landed himself an FA charge after accusing referee Andy D'Urso of having a vendetta against Leeds, and Wise was charged with misconduct after being sent to the stands during an ill-tempered 1-1 draw at Gillingham. It was a result that cost Leeds their 100 per cent record, a club record-breaking eighth straight league win from the start of the season and more besides. Wise's dismissal came between a first-half red card for Trésor Kandol and a second-half dismissal for Jermaine Beckford, and after the match he filed a complaint against the referee, accusing him of using abusive language towards him, 'At the end of the game the referee told me to "f off". I think it is totally and utterly unacceptable, and we as a club will be reporting him. I have three witnesses who are going to back me up.' Not only was Wise's complaint dismissed due to insufficient evidence, but he also received his own charge of using abusive language towards the referee which resulted in a three-match touchline ban and £5,000 fine.

Despite their misdemeanours in the last game of the month, Wise picked up his second consecutive Manager of the Month award, and Kandol picked up the Player of the Month prize, but that was scant consolation. The loss of Leeds's two star strikers to suspension was compounded by injuries to the other frontmen in the squad. Leon Constantine was still a few weeks from fitness and Tore André Flo just couldn't stay fit –

the seven-year wait to see him in a Leeds shirt seemed to have come a few years too late. Wise acted swiftly by bringing in two emergency loan signings to plug the gap: Wayne Andrews and Mark De Vries.

Andrews was a journeyman lower-league striker, on his third loan since signing for Coventry City a year earlier, while De Vries had a slightly better pedigree having played, but ultimately failed, in the Championship and the Dutch Eredivisie. These were two strikers who could never have dreamed of playing for such an illustrious club, but Wise was thankful to have them on board for the midweek trip to Oldham.

With my mates all in their mid-20s the vast majority were footloose and fancy free, resulting in a decent squad of match-goers. Yet Paul and I were the only constants, but Rick usually joined us and the three of us made the trip across the Pennines to Boundary Park, where Leeds had a dismal record. They hadn't won there since 1986 and their only other victory at Oldham had been back in 1928. It was a dreary old-school ground that looked very sorry for itself, befitting of the weather on a cold and wet Lancashire night.

Leeds were allocated the biggest and most modern stand behind the goal, and almost 5,000 travelling fans made it sound like a home game, as they always did. It would become a welcome feature of life in League One; the hosts would never balk at giving Leeds an enormous number of tickets, even if it meant risking the ignominy of the away fans outnumbering the home fans. Maximising gate receipts was more important than saving face.

The loan rangers both started, and both missed decent chances to win a poor game of third-tier football. A tepid display by United seemed destined to yield a single point in a 0-0 bore when Wise brought on Ian Westlake for Alan Thompson with only seconds of injury time remaining. 'We can only lose it now,' I said to Paul, as Oldham launched the last attack of the game, but when the attack broke down the final whistle didn't blow and suddenly Seb Carole was charging down the left wing in front of us. Carole managed to gain half a yard on the full-back and dig out a great cross to the far post which was met by the boot of Westlake, arriving in the box to hammer the ball gloriously into the top corner. What a moment! The Leeds fans went bananas, their team had stolen all three points with the last kick of the match, and what a goal to do it with. The celebrations afterwards were so euphoric that I almost gave in and chanted Wise's name along with the travelling fans. Almost.

Four days later, Yeovil Town came to Elland Road and frustrated the hosts for 89 minutes, but for the fifth time in ten games this season Leeds won all three points in the closing stages. Jonathan Douglas's deep cross was headed home by De Vries, sparking another exuberant Elland Road Shuffle as the fans who packed the gangway at the top of N11 surged down the stairs, falling all over each other in manic celebration. If Wise couldn't take all the credit for the 'us against the world' mentality, he could surely be entirely credited for the 'never say die' attitude of his team. It was clear to see these players would run through walls for each other.

> *Jermaine Beckford: 'The squad at that time was so tight. We weren't just colleagues, we were mates. We'd go to each other's houses after training, go out to eat with all the boys and their missuses, we had an understanding of each other outside the football world and that built such a close connection. It's a cliché, but it was like an extended family.'*

At the final whistle the Kop again saluted the management team who were making amends for the previous season's calamitous relegation. I still couldn't bring myself to join in but, with nine wins in ten games and more last-minute winners than goals conceded, I was loving life in League One.

———

Leeds United 4 Millwall 2

Matchday 13 of 46
Elland Road (30,319)

> *'I've always had a great relationship with Ken Bates and Dennis Wise, and I base that on how they've been with me, the doors they've opened for me and the advice they've given me as well.' – Jermaine Beckford*

The management team weren't the only 'Chelsea scum' winning over the supporters. The chairman received a letter of apology from Ray Fell, chairman of the Leeds United Supporters' Club, who made it clear he was 'wholeheartedly behind Ken Bates'. Leeds were united again, and the fans were flocking to Elland Road. League One Leeds boasted the highest average attendance in the whole Football League, higher too than six Premier League clubs.

The attendances had increased in each game up until the visit of Yeovil, but a crowd of just under 28,000 was still impressive, as was the turnout of over 29,000 for the visit of Leyton Orient, on the same day that Leeds Rhinos were competing in rugby league's Super League Grand Final. It was an eventful day for the city and an eventful day for Seb Carole. With Leeds trailing 1-0 the pacy French winger managed to get the Leyton Orient goalscorer sent off for an innocuous elbow, then he scored the equaliser with a lovely curling strike into the top corner, and with time running out Carole won a soft penalty to give United the chance of claiming another late victory. With no specifically allocated penalty taker, Trésor Kandol took the responsibility, and the advice of top scorer Jermaine Beckford.

Jermaine Beckford: 'I said to him, "Look, if you're going to take it, firstly, score. Secondly, go down the middle because the keeper's going to dive. And thirdly, give it a bit of welly." He absolutely punted that thing, but it seemed like he was wearing Doc Marten boots!'

Kandol's penalty sailed aimlessly over the bar, condemning Leeds to a disappointing 1-1 draw. With the Grand Final kicking off in an hour, thousands of fans dashed straight from Elland Road to Old Trafford, and the 71,000 inside the home of our bitter enemies saw the Rhinos upset the odds by thrashing St Helens 33-6. Having only won two trophies in the past 30 years, this was a momentous victory which helped to build the positive momentum in Leeds, and it launched the hero status of Kevin Sinfield and Rob Burrow, who would become legends of the sport over the next decade, and legends of the city for ever more.

The following week, Kandol made amends for his missed penalty by scoring a 79th-minute winner at Brighton. United were soaring up the table and had the chance to move into the play-off places when Millwall arrived at Elland Road at the end of October. The game marked the anniversary of the appointment of Wise and Poyet, and in his programme notes Bates paid tribute in bizarre fashion, 'They inherited a mess on and off the field but just got on with it and today our position speaks for itself.' Leeds were tenth in League One, Ken! Perhaps Bates was referencing the club's position in 'The REAL League One Table', which was printed in every matchday programme; however, even in the chairman's alternate reality, Leeds might have been top of the league by nine points, but they were top of the worst level of football they had ever competed in.

A heated rivalry between Leeds and Millwall had quickly formed since the Whites plunged from the Premier League, mainly due to the London club's fans routinely celebrating the deaths of two Leeds supporters, Christopher Loftus and Kevin Speight, who were brutally murdered the night before a UEFA Cup semi-final in Istanbul just a few years earlier. Thus, for the first time in 2007/08, Elland Road welcomed a crowd of over 30,000. The match was marred by hooliganism, with the Millwall fans smashing the windows of the coaches transporting them from the train station to the ground, and when they arrived it took a significant police effort to nullify violence as Leeds hooligans attacked.

On the pitch, Leeds treated the bumper crowd to their best performance of the season. After an hour's play they had cruised to a 4-0 lead and the points were in the bag. Or were they? Having only let in two goals in the last nine matches, Casper Ankergren conceded two in ten minutes to give the home fans a scare, but the game ended 4-2 and Wise's men were up to sixth, just four points off top spot. With 35 points from a possible 39, United had exploded out of the blocks.

David Prutton: 'I'm not sure if we were a great team, but we were a great bunch of players together. It was a really good dressing room with a melting pot of different personalities, and the adversity at the start of the season bonded us together. Dennis instilled his strong mentality within us, we had character and personality and that can take you a long way.'

Carlisle United 3 Leeds United 1

Matchday 14 of 46
Brunton Park (16,668)

'Gus was well liked within the squad. There's no doubt him leaving had a big impact on us.' – Casper Ankergren

Gus Poyet's absence from the dugout during the Millwall game hadn't gone unnoticed, but it still seemed to come like a bolt from the blue when he was announced as Juande Ramos's assistant manager at Tottenham Hotspur. Dennis Wise claimed to have had his arms, legs and balls cut off before the season had started; now some people suggested he had lost the brains of the operation. Apparently, Gus took all the training sessions and was the genius behind the near perfect results, while Wise was just a frontman. There was no truth in the rumours according to the players.

> *Casper Ankergren: 'Dennis was always on the training pitch. Gus had a really good football brain but him and Dennis were a good mixture. They looked at football differently, but they were similar characters.'*

Losing Poyet was undoubtedly a major blow, though Ken Bates glossed over it in typically overstated fashion, 'We are here to build, to take on the so-called greats. I can do it with Dennis Wise as the manager, Shaun Harvey as our chief executive and myself, and have a management team to be the envy of football.'

For Bates, the key to reaching the top was to maximise the non-footballing revenue streams available to him, and his masterplan was to build an arcade, hotel and conference centre on the spare space around Elland Road. Bates was always very transparent when it came to his business plans, but his focus on off-field matters ahead of football did not go down well with the supporters. 'Leeds United cannot compete at the highest level if we only take income on home matchdays,' said Bates, who often seemed oblivious to the fact Leeds were in League One. Another example of this was his response to the council when they refused to help finance the stadium redevelopment: 'OK, but don't complain when you have a football team stuck in the upper echelons of the Championship.'

Before Leeds got stuck in the Championship they would need to escape League One, and to help them do so Wise wasted no time in getting himself a new genius, Dave 'Harry' Bassett, who had done well as Wimbledon manager 20 years earlier but little since. As well as Bassett, Wise had also added another genius, if you believed the internet. In 2007 the internet was so young that people hadn't yet become so cynical, and Filipe da Costa's YouTube highlights reel was so impressive that nobody seemed to wonder why Ionikos had loaned him to Athlitiki Enosi Larissa for the previous season. Da Costa had joined Leeds at the end of August but a dispute between him and his former club led to a tantalising wait for FIFA to clear the transfer and allow the new messiah to begin his Elland Road career. Two months later, approval had finally been granted and da Costa was named on the bench for the trip to Carlisle United. Paul, Rick and I were trembling with excitement as we hurtled across the M66.

It was my first return to Carlisle since the 'Great Flood' of 2005. I loved my many weeks spent in Cumbria; the people were the salt of the earth and faced the crisis like absolute trojans. Their football club was in non-league back then, but less than three years later Carlisle were sitting proudly on top of League One and looking well capable of achieving a third promotion in four years. This would be a dangerous match for Leeds, but victory would move them within a point of the division's pace-setters, a position nobody could have envisaged this early in the season.

Once in the ground we took our place on the small, open-air terrace behind the goal. Entertaining Leeds United was clearly a big occasion for the city, and the old ground was packed to the rafters and buzzing with excitement. Jermaine Beckford's first-half strike dampened the atmosphere, and at half-time all was looking rosy – Carlisle may have been top of the league, but they were just another team that couldn't compete with the mighty Leeds. By the end the outlook was very different. A three-goal second-half blitz had stunned the visitors, and even the introductions of da Costa and Leon Constantine couldn't stem the tide. Carlisle ran out 3-1 winners and the rafters around Brunton Park were ringing. Not since the 1980s had their team been on such a high.

Leeds's 13-match unbeaten start to the season was over (unlucky for some), but the players and staff still huddled on the pitch at the final whistle, with Wise desperate to convince everybody it was business as usual. It certainly seemed that way as Leeds bounced back from the loss at Carlisle in impressive style. Braces from Trésor Kandol and Beckford helped Leeds to two victories in four days, which took the Whites to within two points of Carlisle again. However, these were the only victories in a month fraught with turbulence.

Off the pitch there was more frustration for Bates as the FA continued to stonewall his pleas for their help in the points deduction saga. Football's governing body seemed determined not to become embroiled in the dispute, and their latest rejection came when Leeds requested they refer the case to the High Court. Bates wasn't done yet, and his next move was to request an independent arbitration proceeding, in accordance with FA regulations. 'We will continue to pursue this matter step by step,' read a club statement, but every month that passed made a successful outcome less likely.

On the pitch, there was a humiliating FA Cup first round exit to League Two Hereford, a match that was humiliating enough just to be involved in; the first time the club had ever competed before the third round. There was also a humiliating home defeat to Bury in the Football League Trophy, a competition that was also humbling enough just to be involved in, and November ended with a humiliating defeat in the league, 1-0 at lowly Cheltenham Town. Leeds dominated and led the shot count 19-1 before conceding a late winning goal to a superb long-range lob. For Leeds it was a taste of their own medicine, having scored so many late winners themselves.

> *David Prutton: 'My overriding memory of Cheltenham was walking out and seeing two-thirds of the ground in white shirts. The Cheltenham players were like, "Where's our lot? Oh, they're over there in the corner!" That was the moment it really hit home that, yes, this might be a different incarnation of Leeds United, but these fans really do care. You really felt that energy.'*

It was only the second league defeat of the season, but alarm bells were ringing. United had only won two of the seven games since the great Gus Poyet left.

———

Leeds United 4 Huddersfield Town 0

Matchday 19 of 46
Elland Road (32,501)

> *'The footprint Gus had left on us, as a squad, as a team and as individuals, was massive.' – Jermaine Beckford*

Dennis Wise refused to accept Gus Poyet's departure as the cause of a downturn in results; instead he blamed tiredness in the camp. It had indeed been a long and gruelling season already, with the off-field distractions surely not helping the strain, but there was no doubt Leeds had lost something with the breaking up of a genuine managerial duo.

> *Jermaine Beckford: 'The two of them together, they were brilliant. Before games Wisey would give his speech and rile*

everybody up, we'd all be pumped and ready to go out there, then Gus would come over, "Hey boys, boys … Relaaaaax and plaaaaay!" It became a running joke but those little moments make a massive difference, and we did miss that.'

The patchy results in November, coupled with the loss of Poyet, had stifled the feelgood factor at Elland Road, resulting in the smallest crowd of the season for the visit of bottom club Port Vale. It may not have been a fixture that caught the imagination, but it presented the perfect opportunity for Leeds to bounce back into form and the 20,000 who bothered to turn up saw a comfortable 3-0 win. Three points, three goals, and a first clean sheet since October was the perfect way to lift spirits heading into the West Yorkshire derby.

Sadly, I had to miss the Huddersfield game, although this was perhaps a blessing in disguise as my presence seemed to have a curiously positive effect on the Terriers. I had been to lots of matches with my Huddersfield-supporting friends, Billy and Edwin, without ever seeing them fail to win. Actually, there was one time they didn't win, a 0-0 draw with Mansfield at the Millennium Stadium in Cardiff (shudder), which Huddersfield won on penalties to secure promotion back to League One.

The reason for my absence was a lads' trip to Las Vegas, and being 5,000 miles away from Huddersfield Town seemed to do the trick. Leeds thrashed their Yorkshire neighbours 4-0 in front of Elland Road's largest attendance of the season. The resounding win was nice retribution as the Huddersfield fans had defaced the Billy Bremner statue on the night before the game, covering it in blue paint. This despicable act was even more heinous considering it was carried out on the ten-year anniversary of Bremner's death. United were ably assisted by some weak goalkeeping from youngster Alex Smithies, but with back-to-back wins, seven goals scored and none conceded, the feelgood factor was well and truly back at Elland Road.

The next three games yielded a steady total of five points, although without more last-gasp goals it would only have been one. Alan Thompson's injury time free kick earned a point at Walsall, via a deflection off the head of Ian Westlake, who was either trying to get out of the way or stooping to score a brilliant training ground goal (my money's on the former). A serious knee injury for Jonathan Douglas compounded a difficult night for Dennis Wise, but as the door closed on one Jonathan it opened for another, and teenager Howson took his chance with an impressive midfield display in the next game against Bristol Rovers. To great amusement, Howson was credited with the 86th-minute winning goal by the stadium announcer at Elland Road. In fairness, it was such a strange goal that nobody knew who scored it or how, but everyone knew it wasn't Howson as he wasn't anywhere near the action.

> *Jonny Howson: 'Now you mention it I do remember that. It was funny because my dad used to back me for first and last goalscorer, and he actually got paid out because it went down as my goal!'*

Yet another last-gasp goal rescued a point from the Boxing Day trip to Hartlepool, and although there could be no disguising another disappointing performance, the draw was enough to send Leeds to the top of the league, if only for a couple of hours before Swansea overtook them. The next match was set up perfectly.

———

Swansea City 3 Leeds United 2
Matchday 23 of 46
The Liberty Stadium (19,010)

> *'I knew he'd done me straight away. He wasn't going for the ball, he was just out to do me.' – Jonny Howson*

The trip to Swansea marked the halfway stage in the League One campaign. With 52 points already won – before deduction adjustments – Leeds were nicely on course to hit Dennis Wise's ambitious target of 105 points collected to win the title and arrived in South Wales knowing victory would leapfrog them above their hosts to the summit of the table. What a remarkable feat that would be.

Although Leeds had overcome them comfortably at Elland Road, the league table showed that Swansea were a decent outfit, with a beautifully tidy record of 12 wins, four draws and four defeats yielding a total of 40 points from their 20 games, and a plus 20 goal difference. With hindsight, however, this was an outstanding League One team. They were managed by future Belgium manager Roberto Martínez, in his first season in management, and their squad contained several players who would eventually help establish the club in the Premier League: Joe Allen, Leon Britton, Àngel Rangel, and future Leeds manager Garry Monk. They also had future Leeds winger Andy Robinson in the form of his life, and one of the most prolific strikers in the league, Jason Scotland.

I drove to the game with Paul, Rick, and Cowling, and watched as Leeds fell 3-1 behind during a breathless first half. Robinson opened the scoring with a superb free kick in the opening minutes, but within the blink of an eye Jermaine Beckford had scored another fantastic goal to add to his ever-growing collection. Having latched on to a weak back-header by the defender, from the tightest of angles Beckford managed to lob the keeper expertly into the net in front of us with an astonishing finish. Ten minutes later Monk rose to head home a corner and restore his team's advantage.

Leeds then assumed a numerical advantage when Swansea were reduced to ten men following a deliberately diabolical foul on Jonny Howson, which led to angry scenes on the pitch as the teenager was stretchered off.

Jonny Howson: 'He came in the dressing room to apologise while I was on the treatment table, claiming to have gone for the ball and all that. I told him where to go. I'd have had more respect for him if he'd apologised for losing his head, because that's part and parcel of football, emotions run high.'

A topsy-turvy half ended with Scotland powering through a feeble back line to extend the lead in injury time, and the timing of the goal was almost as infuriating as the defending. Trailing 3-1 to ten men set up an intriguing second half, which became mouthwatering when Alan Thompson scored a mirror image of Robinson's free kick within a minute of the restart. Thompson was inches away from repeating the trick shortly after, but this time his free kick struck the post. This further raised the hopes of the travelling army, the adrenaline was pumping and we sensed a stunning victory.

It wasn't to be. Leeds's performance deteriorated as their desperation grew. Swansea regained their composure, and even with ten men looked the more likely to score. When the final whistle blew they had deservedly condemned Leeds to their third defeat of the season, and extended their lead at the top. Despite another setback, being third at the turn of the year was still miraculous, and this sentiment oozed out of an unfazed Dennis Wise, 'I thought Swansea played very well, they are a good team. It was an entertaining game, and being honest, they deserved to win.'

You may have suspected we had a long and miserable journey home, but the defeat was overshadowed by the relief of avoiding getting our heads kicked in. Swansea was a rough place, rougher than I'd anticipated, and despite having first-hand experience of how crazy the Cardiff fans were, for some reason I expected better from their Welsh neighbours.

With reckless disregard for our own safety, the four of us slipped through the line of police that was holding us outside the ground while the Swansea fans dispersed, and headed straight for the car. Within minutes we were confronted by a dozen Welsh hooligans. We were four-strong, dressed in the stupidly expensive clobber that hooligans and wannabes pride themselves in, and we were caught like rabbits in headlights when one of the group asked us, 'Where are you lads from?' Rick is lauded for his excellent impressions and decided to take the lead, but there was no showboating, he played it with his straightest bat. 'Wales,' he replied, in his finest Welsh accent. The reply was predictable, 'Where in Wales?' Rick went on the attack, 'Wales!' He repeated his answer in a tone that suggested they were stupid for asking, and incredibly, the gang let us be and we continued on our merry way to the car. Surely they weren't being nice, they must have just been *that* stupid.

––––

Crewe Alexandra 0 Leeds United 1

Matchday 26 of 46
Gresty Road (6,771)

> *'Dennis told me to be diplomatic but I didn't understand what he meant, I just said, "Yeah, yeah, don't worry, leave the TV stuff to me." Bad idea! I'd never had any media training; I was a wild cannon!' – Jermaine Beckford*

To call January turbulent would be an understatement. For once Ken Bates was not at the centre of it, but he was still causing background noise. The 15 points had become a personal obsession of his, it was now into its fifth month of complaint and the FA were still dragging their feet, so Bates decided drastic action was called for and threatened to sue the Football League. 'The more our legal team have dug into the matter, the more shambolic the administration of both the Football League and Football Association makes it essential that our grievance is aired before a truly independent body, namely the High Court,' he said. Bates still refused to print the proper League One table in the matchday programme, which also listed 'Football League' in the squad list as number 'minus 15', and the club continued to promote the exploits of a racehorse called Minus Fifteen.

Bates was also battling with the council over planning permission for his Chelsea Village-style project at Elland Road. I guess we'll never know if hotels, arcades and nice shiny exteriors would have helped the team claim three points against Oldham; all we know is without these vanity items the team fell to an abysmal 3-1 defeat. With Jonny Howson injured from the disgraceful foul at Swansea, Wise partnered Alan Thompson with Radostin Kishishev in midfield, two ageing players with little left in their tanks. Neither lasted an hour, and the Elland Road crowd were nonplussed as three goals flew past Ankergren in the space of 12 first-half minutes. Substitute Leon Constantine pulled a goal back within seconds of his half-time introduction, but later broke his arm, and with all substitutes already used Leeds were down to ten men. The Latics became the first team to beat Leeds in the league at Elland Road for ten months.

> David Prutton: 'Given that we'd come from minus 15, the Leeds fans may have thought we should've continued to smash the league to pieces but that was never going to be the case. We were a team of League One players, playing for a team that had just been relegated, so there was always going to be inconsistency. I guess the season started to even itself out.'

It had been a thoroughly miserable Christmas period, so for the visit of Northampton Town Dennis Wise rang the changes. The last signing of the summer transfer window, 20-year-old centre-back Paul Huntington, was finally given his first league start, as was the first signing of the winter window, 22-year-old playmaker Neil Kilkenny, whose orchestration of Oldham's shock win at Elland Road four days earlier had convinced Wise to part with £150,000 of Bates's precious money.

Jermaine Beckford: 'We played Oldham on the Saturday and Killer [Kilkenny] was yapping on at me the whole game. We went into a 50-50 and absolutely smashed each other, then squared up, yelling at each other. Then on Monday we bloody sign him! And the first thing he said when he comes into the dressing room, "I'm gonna set you up for so many goals!" We had a great relationship after that.'

Homegrown youngster Ben Parker also came in at left-back, making his second league start, but it was the homegrown right-back, Frazer Richardson, who stole the headlines by setting Leeds on their way to a 3-0 victory with a wonderful solo goal.

It was a nice way to head into a nine-day break, during which the club worked very hard to strengthen the squad. First through the door was Northampton's 20-year-old midfielder Bradley Johnson, signed for a whopping £250,000. It was a dream move for Johnson, and a different world to his previous experiences.

Bradley Johnson: 'In my first week at Thorp Arch I was blown away. The amazing facilities, the quality of the players and the levels of preparation, I'd never known anything like it. That was amazing for me, being a young kid.'

Wingers Sebastian Sorsa and Peter Sweeney completed a whole new midfield when added to the already arrived Kilkenny, and Darren Kenton joined on loan from Leicester, adding strength to a defence that was about to be weakened by the absence of Rui Marques during the African Cup of Nations.

Amid the positive additions was speculation that star striker Jermaine Beckford would be leaving. He was attracting interest from the Premier League, but the rumours were put to bed after Beckford's 16th goal of the season secured a 1-0 victory at Crewe. It was a rare appearance on Sky's *Monday Night Football* for Leeds, and in his post-match interview Beckford was asked where he saw his future, amid reported bids from Newcastle. Pointing to his badge in disbelief, Beckford scoffed, 'What shirt am I wearing bruv? Are you being serious?' It was a statement that struck a chord with the Leeds fans. To hear your best player talk about the club with such high regard, despite how low we'd fallen, was music to the ears and immediately quashed any fears that his departure may be imminent.

Jermaine Beckford: 'I had no idea the impact my answer would make, until I went to my local Indian restaurant after the game. Some guy came over and plopped himself right next to me, literally on my chair, and said, "What shirt am I wearing bruv? Mate, that was absolutely brilliant! It was golden, we loved that!" And then he just bounced off.'

Never one to miss a marketing opportunity, Ken Bates immediately had 'What shirt am I wearing bruv?' T-shirts added to the club store.

With credit to Cuddly Ken, the only departures from Elland Road were on Leeds's terms. Wise needed to trim down a bloated squad that had almost doubled in size from the 16 players that started the season, so captain Alan Thompson was sent on loan to Hartlepool and Radostin Kishishev returned to his parent club Leicester City. One player Leeds couldn't shed was Filipe da Costa. It's fair the say the Portuguese winger hadn't pulled up any trees since his arrival at Elland Road, and the initial excitement over his YouTube skills quickly subsided when he was sent off on his only start, in the Football League Trophy defeat to Bury. He clearly wasn't the messiah after all, he was just a very naughty boy. Da Costa hadn't even made the bench since and headed up to Falkirk on trial, but the secret was out, and they didn't want him either.

Jermaine Beckford: 'Filipe da Costa. He lived in the house directly behind pitch one at Thorp Arch. He could literally jump over his garden fence and be the first one in to training, but he was always late! You could see he had a bit of quality, but mentally I don't think he was ready for a move to Leeds United.'

———

Luton Town 1 Leeds United 1
Matchday 28 of 46
Kenilworth Road (9,297)

'Typical Leeds history, everything's going great and then suddenly something happens, and we're back to square one.'
– Casper Ankergren

With successive victories on the board and new signings through the door, spirits were high ahead of a Yorkshire derby with fellow promotion-chasers Doncaster Rovers. There was another bumper crowd of over 30,000 at Elland Road but I wasn't one of them; I was with my mates on a boozy weekend in Florence to celebrate Paul's 24th birthday. We drank and laughed all weekend, a stark contrast to the mood at Leeds which dipped again as the Whites fell to a 1-0 defeat. Wise admitted his sluggish team had been outplayed by opponents who were more zoned in to a Yorkshire derby than the hosts. United's inability to find any consistency was a growing concern.

Next up was Luton away, for which I stayed at home, my new home – a bachelor pad I'd bought with Paul. Well, it wasn't home just yet, I was still living with my parents while we carried out the renovations. It was home for Paul though; he would have been homeless otherwise and had been sleeping there without heating or floorboards (on the ground floor) for the past three months. Ironically, the house had also been flooded and the loss adjuster was due to visit on this Saturday, so Rick and I tuned in to Radio Leeds to listen to the game while waiting for him to arrive, and played heads-up poker on a cardboard box in what would eventually be my bedroom. Round after round of tea and whispers from bakery The Avenue kept our cockles warm, aided by Paul Huntington's opening goal which looked to have secured an important three points. However, a scrappy game ended with a scrappy equaliser in the fourth minute of injury time, and a polystyrene cup of Yorkshire Tea was hurled at the wall in anger (it needed redecorating anyway, although it wouldn't be redecorated for another five years). In the Leeds dressing room at Kenilworth Road there was a very different response to the dropped points by Dennis Wise.

Bradley Johnson: 'I was looking around the dressing room and everyone had their heads down, they were distraught. Dennis Wise walked in and I thought he was going to tear into us for the result, but he said, "What the fuck are you doing? Get your heads up! You started the season on fucking minus 15, you're in an unbelievable position. Get your fucking heads up!" That's what he was like, he was so good at picking the lads up. He told us we were all staying down in London and we all went out for a meal that night, all the players and staff, and forgot about the game, ready to go and win on Tuesday.'

Leeds were still just one point from the automatic promotion spots, but with only six wins in 16 games they had slipped down to fifth and my confidence was waning. In three days they would see out the month with a midweek trip to Southend, but the real drama of January was only just beginning. The day after their team bonding session in London, Dennis Wise gathered his squad together and dropped a bombshell.

> *Bradley Johnson: 'Dennis Wise sat us all down and told the lads something had come up and he was sad to say he was leaving. He told us he loved us and that he was sure we'd go on and get promoted, but this was an opportunity he couldn't turn down and he had to go. I looked around the room and the lads were heartbroken. It was disappointing for me – the manager who signed you leaving two weeks later – but I think it affected the rest of the squad massively, they loved him. That changing room was so close and it was all down to Wisey.'*

On Monday the news was made public knowledge and Dennis Wise had left the manager's job at Elland Road to take a boardroom role as Newcastle United's 'executive director'. According to the official club statement, Wise and his staff would be preparing the team for Tuesday's match at Southend, but the following day Wise was nowhere to be seen and all his staff had quit too, leaving technical director Gwyn Williams to pick up the reins.

> *Casper Ankergren: 'Dennis suddenly leaving for Newcastle set us back. Suddenly we were going into a game without a manager. Everybody was shocked and couldn't understand what was going on. It was a shame to see the manager leave when you are going through the massive project of getting Leeds back up.'*

Unsurprisingly, a beleaguered Leeds team lost 1-0, and a season that had looked so promising just a month earlier had been turned on its head. The mood in the dressing room was despondent.

> *Bradley Johnson: 'There were a lot of older pros in the dressing room and after the game they sat the lads down, and told us this happens in football and we just had to forget about it and kick on. We'd put ourselves in an unbelievable position from where we'd started, and whoever came in next we just had to keep doing what we'd been doing and get out of this league.'*

Leeds United 0 Tranmere Rovers 2

Matchday 30 of 46
Elland Road (24,907)

> *'And remember ... let's stick together this season.'*
> *'Please keep up your support, let's stick together, and see where it takes us.'*
> *'Elland Road is buzzing because we're all in this together. Let's keep that going.'*

The above are a few examples of Dennis Wise's closing sentences from his matchday programme notes in 2007/08, yet at the first sniff of an opportunity the manager had walked out on the club. 'Dennis came in like a whirlwind!' wrote Bates in his next programme notes. 'Like me, unpopular and resented, he did a magnificent job in setting the shape for the renaissance of Leeds United. Thank you Dennis, we owe you nothing except gratitude.' It was a nauseating tribute from a notoriously hostile chairman, finally living up to his 'Cuddly Ken' ironic moniker, at the most annoying time. I did have some gratitude to Wise and if anyone was going to lead Leeds United into the third tier of English football, I was glad it was him.

> *Jermaine Beckford: 'Dennis leaving was a huge blow for me personally. We had a great relationship, we'd both grown up in the same area of London and had a lot in common, and he did so much for my career. I missed the little bits of banter, the jokes, and the advice he would give me, but then we replaced one legend of the game with another.'*

Bates wasted no time in appointing Wise's replacement. Club legend Gary McAllister was interviewed on the same day that Wise left, then the following day he flew to Monaco – where Bates lived in tax exile – to sign his contract. 'You can see that I'm not here for the money,' McAllister allegedly joked to Bates. 'Yes, and neither am I,' was the chairman's deadpan response. It's the way you tell 'em, Ken.

It was a surprise appointment from Bates as not only had McAllister been out of the game for four years, his only previous managerial experience came during 18 months as player-manager at Coventry City, which ended in unthinkable circumstances with McAllister resigning in order to care for his wife, who tragically succumbed to breast cancer. He also had a philosophy that was very different to Wise. McAllister was a cultured midfielder and liked his teams to play in a similar manner, which would mean asking the current squad to deviate from the brand of football that had taken the division by storm in the early months of the season.

> *Bradley Johnson: 'The team had been very direct under Wise, a team of men who knew what they were doing, with Kandol and Becks scoring goals for fun. Some of the lads thought we should stick to what had worked over the first*

half of the season, but McAllister wanted to do it his way and get us playing free-flowing football.'

Regardless of the stark change in style, Bates insisted McAllister was his first-choice replacement for Wise, 'I'm not backward in making unpopular decisions, but on this occasion I hope it's popular because it's both constructive and logical.' Bates continued, 'I said 20 years ago I wanted my team to be cheered off for entertainment and I want that to happen here. I think Gary will give us that.'

McAllister had won the last First Division title as a player at Leeds, but when he left for Coventry the fans were furious and he had been roundly booed at Elland Road ever since. All that negativity was immediately forgotten the minute he replaced Wise in the hotseat; we finally had a Leeds United-minded person in a leading role at the club. 'There is no doubt in my mind that the Leeds fans are among the best in the world,' said a delighted McAllister. 'When they get going, Elland Road is an intimidating place to play and that is what we have got to create in the home games we have left.'

McAllister's first week at the club was a whirlwind. From Monaco he flew back to Yorkshire and took his first training session the next day, which also happened to be transfer deadline day. Leeds had already made Darren Kenton's loan from Leicester permanent, which became a double swoop when the Foxes' young left-back, Alan Sheehan, arrived on loan. To be fair to Bates it had been quite an ambitious window, and by midnight the club's January outlay had reached an eye-watering £850,000 in transfer fees with the additions of Ľubomír Michalík and Anthony Elding. Michalík was a tall and imposing Slovakian international centre-back, who was returning to the club after an impressive loan spell in the second half of the previous season, while Elding was a striker high on confidence having notched 15 goals already in 2007/08, albeit in the division below. Leeds had been lacking an alternative striking option all season, with injuries ravaging the seasons of Flo and Constantine. Between them they only managed seven starts, and by March they would both be gone.

Like Dennis Wise, McAllister's first League One opponent was Tranmere Rovers, but the new manager's reign got off to the worst possible start. All four deadline-day signings were included in McAllister's first selection, but three of them were replaced in the second half as Leeds fell to a 2-0 defeat. Elding looked especially off the pace, so it added to the frustration that former Whites striker Ian Moore secured the points on his Tranmere debut, doubling the lead to the delight of his new manager, his old man, Ronnie Moore, whose team leapfrogged Leeds and knocked them out of the play-off places.

Having bemoaned a poor match, McAllister saw a 'massive improvement' in his second game at Northampton but he failed to pick up his first win as Adebayo Akinfenwa cancelled out Jonny Howson's opener. Having only been in the job a matter of days, McAllister found himself in a sticky position. Leeds had only collected two points from the previous 15 available and their season was at a crossroads. The surge to the top of the table was now a distant memory, and the stark reality of life in League One had bitten.

———

Leeds United 1 Nottingham Forest 1

Matchday 32 of 46
Elland Road (29,552)

'To go from playing one way and getting results, to changing the style and not getting results, it's always going to affect the mood in the camp, especially when you find yourselves slipping out of the play-off places.' – Bradley Johnson

Having seen his request for an arbitration tribunal rejected by the FA, Ken Bates followed through on his threat and issued a High Court writ against the Football League, seeking a ruling that they had not complied with their own regulations when docking the points. It was his last throw of the dice and it worked; the Football League granted Bates his arbitration tribunal and a three-man panel would sit to discuss the merits of the 15-point deduction 'before the end of the season'. It had taken six months, but there was finally a glimmer of light at the end of the tunnel.

Next up for McAllister was Nottingham Forest under the lights at Elland Road, the marquee fixture on the League One calendar. Midweek matches were magical back when Leeds were entertaining the best teams in the country and beyond, but in the lower leagues they were a different kettle of fish. You often got the sense that nobody even wanted to be there, and even the most die-hard of fans were there out of duty rather than excitement. This night felt like a return to the glory days.

Playing Nottingham Forest, you could almost pretend it was a top-flight clash, plus, the fixture took extra significance due to the intrinsic links to Brian Clough, the outspoken and enigmatic manager who had clashed with Leeds in the 1960s and '70s, then managed them for 44 days. 'Old Big 'Ead' had served up my first taste of defeat at Elland Road, on his final visit on 5 December 1992, and amazingly, the attendance for this midweek League One match against the same opponent attracted 188 more people than that Premier League clash had, when Leeds were the reigning champions of England.

Apart from feeling like a big game, this was a big game, with Leeds sitting four points behind third-placed Forest who also had two matches in hand. There were 15 games still to go, but Leeds couldn't afford to lose if they harboured hopes of a renewed bid for automatic promotion. McAllister's team was similar to Wise's in personnel but the football was very different, with the new manager looking to cultivate a team that would play their way out the division rather than fight their way out. Unsurprisingly then, the tweak was in midfield, where Jonny Howson was brought in to partner Andy Hughes, who McAllister made stand-in captain, and clearly admired greatly, 'Hughesy? He'll play anywhere, bless him. He just loves football. I love him.'

With Hughes it was love, but McAllister's feelings for Howson may have verged on lust. This was a talented young midfielder that the new manager could take under his wing and mould in his image. Howson was the latest product from the Thorp Arch academy and referring to him as a 'local lad' barely cuts the mustard – growing up, he could see Elland Road from his bedroom window. Naturally, he was Leeds through and through, and there could be no better manager for him to learn from. McAllister made Howson a pivotal part of his team, at the point of a midfield diamond where he would be expected to get in the box and among the goals, which was music to the ears of Jermaine Beckford.

Jermaine Beckford: 'Jonny Howson was one of those players that I absolutely adored playing with. His delivery was unbelievable, he had a great engine, just kept on running, and he would never pull out of a 50-50 either – I know that first-hand!'

The match lived up to the hype, as did the atmosphere. It was the most vociferous Elland Road had been since the rip-roaring start to the season, a noise worthy of any level of football. McAllister's new style of play finally clicked and it was wonderful to see the passing and movement from defence to attack, led by a non-stop performance from David Prutton. Against his old club, 'Prutts' enjoyed his best game since arriving at Elland Road, dictating play and popping up here, there and everywhere to help out his team-mates. His rise in form had earned him the adulation of the Leeds fans, who nicknamed him 'Jesus', owing to his long brown hair and divine performances.

David Prutton: 'I was just loving life at Leeds. After a couple of tough years it was amazing to be playing for such a big club. Being a Yorkshireman, living back in the area was great. I was seeing my parents and family regularly and it was a time of my life when I could just throw myself into the football.'

Despite Leeds's excellent display, Forest opened the scoring 20 minutes from time and looked to have stolen all three points. The Elland Road faithful were undeterred, they had seen enough to remain faithful and roared Leeds on, and with the clock ticking down Wes Morgan yanked Trésor Kandol's shirt and referee Mark Halsey generously pointed to the spot. Rather than sucking the ball into the net, the Kop may just have sucked the air through the ref's whistle. It was a great relief to see the penalty awarded, and after Kandol's horror penalty earlier in the season it was just as pleasing to see Jermaine Beckford with the ball in his hands.

Jermaine Beckford: 'I knew I'd score loads of goals so let Tres be on the first penalty, but told him I'd be on them as soon as he missed one. He took one and missed it, and from then on it was, "Right where's that ball, I'm on it!"'

Beckford converted the spot-kick in expert fashion, earning a point that was the least United deserved. Leeds had lost more ground on the play-off places but I left the ground feeling happier than I had in months. It was so refreshing to have a manager and a brand of football that we could be proud of. Now all we needed were some wins.

Crewe at home presented the perfect opportunity for McAllister to claim his first victory, and the manager must have been delighted when Kandol scored at Elland Road for the first time since the day Leeds reached zero points. The goal was a nod to the previous regime; it was late, direct, and created by Seb Carole, the winger who had lost his place in the team since the January transfer flurry. But it only rescued another point, and with just two wins in the 12 games since Christmas, Leeds had dropped down to ninth place.

———

Leeds United 2 Walsall 0

Matchday 38 of 46
Elland Road (19,095)

> *'To change your philosophy in the middle of a season is not easy. McAllister had the players to play that type of football, but it just took time.'* – Casper Ankergren

On the eve of the next game at Swindon Town, Leeds Rhinos backed up their Super League victory by beating Melbourne Storm 11-4 to win rugby league's World Club Challenge in front of Elland Road's biggest crowd of the season, 33,204. It was a much-needed boost for the city, and the next day its football club grabbed a much-needed victory, McAllister's first at the fifth attempt. Having waited all winter for a goal a second arrived in quick succession for Trésor Kandol, who followed up his equaliser against Crewe with the only goal of the game.

A 2-0 victory over relegation-bound Bournemouth followed, with no small thanks to two January signings who were starting to make a big impression. After struggling with injuries, Neil Kilkenny had now made it into the team, and being a lovely passer of the ball, his job was to pull the strings.

Bradley Johnson, meanwhile, was a powerful presence down the left, with a terrific spring that made him a great outlet from goal kicks, and a dangerous presence in the box. With Prutton in top form and Howson full of confidence, United had a settled and functioning midfield quartet who all contributed to the goals that saw off Bournemouth. Prutton's measured up-and-under had created the first goal for Johnson, and Howson created the second by jinking around Max Gradel before feeding Kilkenny, who whipped in a deadly finish at the Kop end. Howson wasn't surprised to see the new midfielders thriving.

Jonny Howson: 'You could see Brad and Kilkenny had the determination to do well, and despite their age they both had the right attitude to be able to play for Leeds United, and to play in League One. There's a lot of pressure that comes with that, you were expected to win every game and a lot of players couldn't handle it, but those two could.'

Things were looking rosy again. The successive victories pushed Leeds back to the brink of the play-off places and six more points were expected to be added over the next four days with two games against relegation strugglers. But just when McAllister seemed to have turned the corner his team's five-match unbeaten run was ended by Cheltenham Town, who completed the double over Leeds with a shock 2-1 victory at Elland Road. It was probably the worst league defeat in the club's history, and the weekend trip to rock-bottom Port Vale wasn't much better; in some ways it was even worse.

Our Burke Street bachelor pad was now deemed habitable, and my first Saturday in my new home was spent with Paul and Rick, drinking Henry Weston's cider and playing 'Burke Triathlons' for a tenner (darts, poker, and *FIFA*), while keeping an eye on *Soccer Saturday* as Leeds yo-yoed at Vale Park. After cruising into a 2-0 half-time lead, two goals in two minutes pegged United back, the first of which was a penalty awarded for handball when the ball clearly struck Andy Hughes on the head. New signing Dougie Freedman had scored his debut goal – turning on a sixpence to make it 2-0 – and his second goal restored the lead in the 87th minute, prompting jubilant scenes as we bounced around the living room believing the game was won. It wasn't. Vale picked themselves up from the canvas again and scrambled home a gut-wrenching equaliser right at the death. What a sickener.

One positive despite the dropped points was the performance of Freedman, who had been brought in on loan from Crystal Palace where he enjoyed legendary status having scored over 100 goals in over 300 games for the Eagles. At the age of 33 Freedman was now surplus to requirements at Selhurst Park, but his vast experience was vital to the Leeds squad and his guile was crucial to the team, the Scot linking with the midfield to feed Beckford rather than have him feed off the scraps from Kandol's head. This was the last piece of McAllister's jigsaw; he had now made the team his own.

> *Jermaine Beckford: 'It was a completely different dynamic with Dougie. As much as it was disappointing that my partnership with Tres was coming to an end, I loved having the opportunity to play alongside someone who had made such an impression on the game. It gave me the opportunity to add another string to my bow, and along with Gary McAllister and Steve Staunton, Dougie helped me to become a more rounded player.'*

In the next game against Walsall, broadcast live on Sky on Easter Saturday evening, only four players out of the 11 that had wiped out the 15-point deficit remained in the team: Ankergren, Rui Marques, Prutton and Beckford. By the time kick-off came around Leeds were tenth in the table, only two points ahead of neighbours Huddersfield in 13th, despite having a better goal difference by 41. But Leeds were looking up, not down, and victory would leapfrog the Whites above their opponents, and within two points of the play-offs.

With only eight games of the season remaining this was a genuine six-pointer, yet it attracted the lowest attendance of the campaign as barely 18,000 Leeds fans turned up, supplemented by 1,000 in the away end. It was the first sub-20,000 crowd for a league game at Elland Road in my lifetime supporting the club, and the home supporters embraced the groundbreaking low characteristically, giving birth to a chant that would get lots of airtime over the next decade, 'IF YOU'RE WATCHING ON THE TELLY, WATCHING ON THE TELLY, WATCHING ON THE TELLY YOU'RE A C***!'

The 19,000, and the 'c***s' at home, witnessed a classy performance from McAllister's side. They looked a cut above their play-off rivals and Beckford moved on to 19 goals for the season with two devastating finishes from defence-splitting passes by Kilkenny.

Leeds were on the brink of the play-offs again, but with the arbitration tribunal preparing to discuss the points deduction nobody knew what race they were in. Without knowing how many points Leeds would get back, if any, working out the table was futile, but in the unlikely event that the punishment was quashed entirely they would be shunted into the automatic promotion spots, a point ahead of Carlisle and four clear of Doncaster, with both teams to face at the beginning of April.

Leeds United 3 Carlisle United 2

Matchday 42 of 46
Elland Road (28,530)

*'I thoroughly enjoyed it under McAllister. From travelling with the squad more, to starting the odd game, suddenly I was established in the side, playing for the club I loved.' –
Jonny Howson*

After a difficult winter period Leeds were back on track, finally finding consistency for the first time since the opening months of the season, and Ken Bates rewarded Gary McAllister with a one-year extension to his initial six-month contract. McAllister had only tasted defeat once in ten games since losing his opening match, and his team headed into a potentially vital home clash with second-placed Carlisle United having collected ten points from the last 12 available, without conceding a goal. This run included a potentially vital away win against third-placed Doncaster, though nobody would know how vital until after the arbitration hearing. The 1-0 victory – on Leeds's first visit to the Keepmoat Stadium – was McAllister's most impressive yet, and came courtesy of a brilliant free kick by Alan Sheehan. The young left-back was starting to hit his stride and the winning goal would have done his confidence no harm at all.

There were five games remaining and Carlisle arrived at Elland Road in prime position to take the second automatic promotion spot behind runaway leaders Swansea City. The Cumbrians were six points clear of Doncaster, eight ahead of Southend United and nine in front of Nottingham Forest, who were surely too far adrift. Leeds weren't mathematically out of the running, 15 points behind Carlisle with a game in hand, and an arbitration tribunal as the ace up their sleeve (or a joker at least). More pertinent to McAllister was the race for the play-offs, and with Tranmere on their heels this was a huge game no matter what happened with the arbitration. It was a big match too for Paul Huntington; the Carlisle-born youngster had finally nailed down his place in the team and it would be the biggest occasion of his career. He would be marking his half-cousin, Scott Dobie, too.

It was a bright and sunny spring afternoon and the gangway of N11 was especially packed out as a load of our mates had accompanied Paul and I, including Paul's brother Nige and his girlfriend Becky, who was treated to a raucous debut at Elland Road. All the action was at the Kop end as Carlisle dominated the first half and took a deserved lead into the break, and to Huntington's horror it was Dobie's strike that separated the teams. At half-time we were nervously checking the Tranmere score with our play-off place in jeopardy.

It was a vital moment in the season and McAllister's half-time team talk led to a blistering second-half display. Dougie Freedman levelled within five minutes of the restart, and the Elland Road Shuffle left Becky clinging on to Nige for dear life. Less than ten minutes later there was more carnage when Jonny Howson arrived in the box to prod Leeds in front, but moments later Casper Ankergren spilled a cross at the feet of former Whites loanee Danny Graham, who was never going to miss.

An exhilarating battle continued, with the hosts responding superbly and bombarding the goal at the Kop end. Nige later admitted he was scared about the prospect of Leeds scoring again, and less than ten minutes after Carlisle's equaliser they did just that. After a goalmouth scramble, Freedman fired into the top corner and the N11 gangway went into meltdown. They had seen four goals in 20 minutes and poor Becky was covered in bruises afterwards; to us it was all in a day's work. Huntington was in overdrive too, and directed his celebrations firmly in the direction of the travelling fans of his hometown club, an act that would result in an FA charge and some angry messages from his fellow Cumbrians. 'My girlfriend and sister have had quite a lot of threats, and people have been saying they are going to kill me when I come home,' said a shaken

Huntington after the match. 'The Carlisle fans are within their rights to be angry and not let it go, I just hope they can accept my apology because I'm genuinely sorry for what happened.'

It had been the game of the season, a brilliant advert for League One, and this was reflected in the words of the defeated manager John Ward, whose grace after losing such an important match showed just what a great match it had been, 'It was a cracking game for both sets of fans. Whether you are neutral or not, if you like football then you have had your absolute money's worth.' The excitement of the match had perhaps been heightened because the following week the arbitration tribunal was due to take place, with a result expected by Friday. If results went their way in the courtroom and on the pitch, Leeds's League One adventure would end at Millwall in seven days' time.

———

Millwall 0 Leeds United 2
Matchday 44 of 46
The New Den (13,395)

> *'Even now, it's hard to take in. You're the second youngest ever Leeds United captain, and the other guy's got a statue outside the ground.' – Jonny Howson*

Before all the excitement of the arbitration hearing and a trip to Millwall there was the little matter of the West Yorkshire derby, but the less said about that the better. Jonathan Douglas had recently won back his place at the base of McAllister's midfield diamond, but after two bookings inside 38 minutes he must have feared his season was over. By half-time Huddersfield had also been reduced to ten men, but the hosts prevailed with a single goal 15 minutes from time. Then came the all-important arbitration hearing, which was concluded on time but the outcome was pending, and a decision was only promised before the last game of the season. It was probably always meant to be this way; the agonising uncertainty over the league table would linger right to the end.

Millwall away brought my second trip to the New Den. The first was a frustrating 1-1 draw in March 2005, in which Kevin Blackwell had his team wasting time to secure a point, when only three would keep their slim play-off hopes alive. The journey was almost as frustrating as the match, with the process of getting the Leeds fans to and from South Bermondsey resembling prisoner transfer. It was such a hassle that I vowed never to go to Millwall again, but this time we would not be subjected to all that palaver. Paul and I stayed in London the night before, visiting our friends Macca and Cowling for a night out, which enabled us to get the train to the ground like any 'normal' Millwall fan.

Football in the capital is truly unique, in this continent anyway. With a dozen or so professional clubs competing in the Football League, on Saturdays the London Underground is dominated by football fans shooting through the tube stations. At every stop there were small pockets, or large swarms, and it was enjoyable to be a part of the camaraderie; despite our rivalries, we were all one and the same. Those harmonious feelings instantly dissipated when making our final connection, an overground train to South Bermondsey that was full of Millwall nutcases. We couldn't turn back now, so we tip-toed on to the train hoping to remain inconspicuous, and an uncomfortable journey ensued.

Uncomfortable is fine though, I'd have snapped your hand off for uncomfortable, but we still had one more hurdle to clear and we had no idea it would be so high. We alighted the train and walked towards the ground, surrounded by the enemy. It was a walk which left me longing for the safety of prisoner transfer, but there wasn't a copper in sight. What was in sight sent shivers down my spine, a sign for the away end, which led down a little fenced-off path resembling a chicken run. As soon as we turned down that path the Millwall nutters would all know we were Leeds fans, and God knows what would happen next. We held our breath and briskly turned down the path and braced ourselves, for nothing as it turned out. Perhaps they didn't notice us sloping off, but we didn't look back to check and only exhaled once safely at the turnstiles.

In these days social media was barely a thing. I had only just signed up to Facebook but I hadn't even heard of Twitter, which had launched the year before. Thus, the line-ups would not be delivered by your phone but by the stadium announcer, and on arrival in the upper tier of the away end behind the goal the team news was greeted with raised eyebrows and dropped jaws. Gary McAllister had bestowed the ultimate honour on Jonny Howson, handing him the captain's armband. At the tender age of 19, Howson became the youngest captain of Leeds United since the great Billy Bremner, but it came as no surprise to his team-mates.

> *Jermaine Beckford: 'As a person and as a professional, Jonny Howson was incredible. He was so young, but he was so mature for his age, and he was so hungry and so driven, and he was absolutely determined to be the best that he could be.'*

It was certainly a surprise to Howson.

> *Jonny Howson: 'It's more than you dream of. As a kid growing up in the area you dream of playing for Leeds United, but you never dream of becoming the club's second youngest captain. Three or four years earlier I'd been playing down an age group at Thorp Arch and was almost released because I was too small, now I was captaining the side at Millwall away!'*

Another surprise was Anthony Elding returning to the team, chosen ahead of Trésor Kandol to partner Freedman up front, with Jermaine Beckford injured. Without their talisman it was perhaps no surprise that a dull battle ensued at the New Den, with the main entertainment coming in the stands as the Leeds and Millwall fans abused each other. However, the match was lit up by Jesus himself, aka David Prutton, who fired an 80th-minute volley into the net from the edge of the box to send the Leeds players and fans wild. In the closing stages the game was put to bed by another cult hero of Elland Road, with Andy Hughes scoring his first (and only) goal for the club. It was a lovely goal too, a clinical finish that followed intricate, one-touch build-up play between Howson, Freedman, Johnson and Hughes himself. McAllister must have enjoyed the goal as much as anyone; his persistence with sexy football had come to fruition.

The Leeds fans were held in a car park for what seemed an eternity after the game, but were buoyed by the news of a last-minute Southend goal that defeated Carlisle and sealed the Whites' automatic promotion, pending the safe return of our precious 15 points. We celebrated the feat half-heartedly, as everybody knew that in all likelihood this important win would ultimately beat a big step towards the play-offs, not out of them.

> David Prutton: 'There was an element of hope about getting the points back, and for the Leeds fans that would have been one of the sweetest places to seal promotion. Christ almighty the place would have been smashed to pieces!'

———

Leeds United 2 Gillingham 1

Matchday 46 of 46
Elland Road (38,256)

'We never expected to get any points back. We're Leeds, everyone hates us, the Football League weren't going to do Leeds any favours.' – Bradley Johnson

By the time the penultimate Saturday of the season rolled around there had still been no arbitration ruling, so inevitably, and almost fittingly, and certainly suspiciously, the matter would drag on into the final week. Leeds headed to Yeovil still with work to do in order to guarantee themselves a play-off spot, and a 1-0 win courtesy of another Dougie Freedman goal sealed the deal. Meanwhile, the automatic promotion race had turned into one of the most dramatic I had known, even without the off-field drama of whether Leeds would be thrust into the mix. Carlisle were beaten for the third game running, handing the initiative over to Doncaster who knew victory in their final match would guarantee promotion. A late surge had given Nottingham Forest a chance too, and they were now the main threat to Doncaster having overtaken Carlisle on goal difference. Leeds were seven points back, and their fate, and that of their rivals, would be revealed just two days before the last match.

I spent Thursday, 1 May in my van, driving around Yorkshire, visiting homes that had suffered damage ranging from a leaking radiator to a full house fire, and lots in between. Some days I'd spend much more time driving in the van than I would on jobs, and would pass the time by chatting away with Rick on my 'Parrot' (speaker phone system for the van).

On this day, with the decision of the arbitration panel about to be revealed, I was happy to be left with my own thoughts. It was tantalising to spend the whole day wondering what would become of us, playing out the different scenarios in my mind's eye. Would Saturday be a promotion party? Imagining the scene was delightful, and what a day it would be: Leeds United overcoming the Football League and their compatriots, who had done all they could to ensure we would fail. We didn't need all our points back to be arriving at a celebratory Elland Road on Saturday afternoon; ten would be enough to secure an immediate return to the Championship and four would give us a fighting chance. If we did get all our points back we'd be a point behind Swansea and playing for the League One title!

In the end we got none. Zero. Zilch. The panel agreed there were inconsistencies and a lack of clarity in the Football League's decision, but still let the punishment stand, mainly because Leeds had initially agreed not to appeal, and also because it would be unfair on the other teams to move the goalposts at such a late stage of the season. The procrastinations of the Football League, the FA, and the arbitration panel itself had ultimately sealed our fate. Ken Bates was flabbergasted at the decision but accepted it as he had always promised he would, once the matter had been dealt with by a neutral panel. 'If this is justice, I am a banana,' remarked Bates, closing the whole affair with poetic aplomb.

So we arrived at a boiling-hot, rammed-full Elland Road for a dead rubber, although it wasn't quite that for Gillingham as they were battling to beat the drop and a defeat would relegate them to League Two. As well as voting in favour of our points deduction, Gillingham's chairman had enraged Bates by applauding the decision to uphold Leeds's punishment, so Bates publicly prayed for the 'poetic justice' of the Whites relegating Gillingham and a crowd of almost 40,000, the largest all-seated crowd in Football League history, saw it delivered.

The first-half performance didn't bode well for the play-offs. The players seemed to freeze in front of a full Elland Road and Paul Huntington gave away the first goal with a sloppy back-pass. However, Leeds rallied in the second half and Bradley Johnson fired home a stunning volley to equalise with 20 minutes remaining, a goal he still considers the best of his career.

> *Bradley Johnson: 'I'll never forget that goal. Everybody always talks about the goal I scored against Arsenal a couple of years later, but nobody knows about my Gillingham goal. I have to get the video out to show people!'*

A chaotic season was tidily book-ended when Trésor Kandol scored a late goal to claim a 2-1 victory, just as he had done on the opening day at Tranmere. More significantly, the result condemned Gillingham to relegation, to the delight of the Leeds fans and chairman. Elsewhere, Cheltenham pulled off an improbable win against Doncaster Rovers to save themselves from the drop and allow Nottingham Forest to win a promotion race they were never really a part of until the finishing line.

Leeds's first League One campaign had been truly unique and unforgettable. They had done tremendously well to finish fifth and boasted the largest average attendance in the whole of the Football League, better than all the clubs in the Championship, which ended the season as the fourth-best-supported league in Europe. Leeds's 26,952 average fell short of Manchester City's League One record of 28,261, but I bet City weren't charging Premier League prices! Now all the focus was on the play-offs, and Leeds's opponents would be a wounded and wobbling Carlisle. The whole season was on the line; could Leeds finish the job?

Leeds United 1 Carlisle United 2
Play-off semi-final first leg
Elland Road (36,297)

> *'It was amazing coming out of the tunnel and seeing Elland Road packed out. It was so loud and energetic.' – David Prutton*

Leeds were hot favourites to overcome Carlisle and reach Wembley for the first time since 1996. Not only had they beaten them a month earlier, and collected 11 more points through the season, the Cumbrians were in terrible form having blown a seemingly unassailable position in second place by winning just one of their final eight games. Perhaps if top scorer Joe Garner hadn't ruptured his cruciate ligament and missed the last 14 matches they would have crawled or sprinted over the finish line; instead, Nottingham Forest reeled them in from 12 points behind on 1 April to finish two points ahead on 3 May.

The greatest atmosphere I had ever experienced was the Championship play-off semi-final against Preston in 2006. Elland Road was absolutely electric that night, from well before kick-off, so I was bouncing off the walls in anticipation of this match. As with the Preston tie, I was disappointed Elland Road would host the first leg but delighted it would be under the lights, ensuring a fervent atmosphere. You would never have known it was a Monday night in Leeds; town was rammed as everyone got well oiled for the big match. Once at the ground the atmosphere was indeed electric, so much so that I wasn't disappointed when Leeds were forced to attack the Kop in the first half; surely they could blow Carlisle away.

They could have done, if young goalkeeper Keiren Westwood wasn't in such inspired form. Within the first 15 minutes he had denied Dougie Freedman and Jermaine Beckford with flying saves that were almost a replica of each other. Beckford's effort, especially, seemed in all the way. I had a brilliant view as the ball swerved into the far corner, and I couldn't believe it when Westwood's fingertips diverted the ball around the post.

Westwood wasn't the only visitor on top form, his team-mates were thriving in the partisan atmosphere and almost took the lead when a volley cruelly struck the post. Then they did take the lead when another volley deflected in off Danny Graham's backside. Graham had earlier been denied by a brilliant Ankergren save but the Dane stood no chance with this one. Elland Road was stunned by the goal and their team struggled to rally. Things were to get worse early in the second half when Carlisle's attack danced around the static Leeds defence resulting in an easy second goal. Facing a two-goal deficit after an hour of their home leg, Leeds's promotion hopes were in tatters, and worse still, Jermaine Beckford's night was complete.

Jermaine Beckford: 'I did my ankle in a challenge near the centre circle. To this day my ankle still clicks and cracks from that challenge. I was in a lot of discomfort throughout the game and after an hour I just couldn't go any further. I was gutted.'

As the final whistle approached Carlisle's focus turned to protecting what they had rather than adding to it, which allowed Leeds to build some late pressure. And in the last of six added minutes a high ball into the South Stand goalmouth dropped at the feet of Freedman, who lashed it under Westwood and into the net to restore some hope. Of all the late goals Leeds had scored this season, this was the latest and perhaps the most important, but it was greeted with the most underwhelming response. I actually thought the goal had been disallowed such was the lack of exuberance in the Kop and the lack of celebration from the players, and the final whistle blowing before Carlisle could kick off added to the confusion even more.

Had the final whistle gone before the ball hit the net? The match was over and I wasn't sure what the final score was (if only Bates had replaced the scoreboard instead of building the Legends Lounge). Thankfully Freedman had indeed given

Leeds a fighting chance, preventing the night from being a complete disaster.

You could have expected both managers to be disappointed with the result in the circumstances but Gary McAllister praised his players for sticking with it all the way to the 96th minute, while Carlisle's manager John Ward praised his players for their application, 'We've come to Leeds with a 40,000 crowd baying for blood and have stood up to it exceptionally well. I've got to be happy with a goal lead.'

> *David Prutton: 'I think we were quite nervy that night. Dougie Freedman put it into context though in the dressing room afterwards – we'd not been at our best and we'd not won the game, but there was still another game to come. We owed the fans a decent performance after that first leg, we had to show them we could handle the pressure and deal with the occasion.'*

———

Carlisle United 0 Leeds United 2

Play-off semi-final second leg
Brunton Park (12,873)

> 'What a night. I've not had many other nights like that in my career, there probably hasn't been one.' – Jonny Howson

Playing the semi-final in two midweek games within the same week added extra spice to the tie, but a reduced away allocation meant I was unable to get a ticket and instead would watch in town with the rest of my mates. I took the afternoon off work and Paul, Rick and I started early, supping bottles of Henry Weston's eight per cent rocket-fuel to get us in the mood, before heading to The Alex on a sunny Thursday afternoon. By kick-off the pub was absolutely rammed, and my mates were all packed into our own little pen, which in day-to-day use was the disabled exit, directly under the projector and directly in front of the screen. We had acquired the perfect spot.

I always go through the same cycle of emotions in the build-up to a mammoth game, starting with extreme pessimism. This is clearly a defence mechanism, trying to accept defeat in advance to cushion the blow when 'the inevitable' happens. As kick-off approaches the enthusiasm builds and I can no longer control my excitement, especially if booze is involved, and especially when that booze is Henry Weston's rocket fuel. By kick-off I'm terrified of the worst again, but on this occasion the fear lasted barely ten minutes thanks to an early goal by Jonny Howson. It was a lovely goal too. Howson picked up possession from Beckford's flick-on and fed Dougie Freedman out on the left, then continued his run into the box and Freedman found him expertly. Howson took the ball on his chest and rifled a clinical left-footed strike into the far corner of the net, right in front of the sun-drenched Leeds fans. Leeds were level and the pub erupted. Game on! It was the perfect start, but now that it was all to play for the fear returned. At half-time my mates were buoyant and couldn't wait for the second half, but the situation was too critical for me to join in with any camaraderie.

The evening sun had set and the second half started in the darkness of night, adding to the tension. Both teams carved out chances but Westwood was once again on top form in the Carlisle goal, and when Bradley Johnson's header finally beat him the woodwork came to the rescue. I couldn't help feeling it wasn't going to be our night. The aggregate score was still level as the clock ticked towards the 90th minute, and the fourth official signalled for only one minute of added time, something I hadn't seen before and haven't seen since. Perhaps the ref took pity on the players, who were already out on their feet and still had another 30 minutes of extra time to play. Or did they?

Leeds had possession and launched one last attack. Hughes played the ball up to Freedman, standing 25 yards out and with his back to goal. With one touch, a beautiful flick with the outside of his boot, Freedman laid the ball perfectly to Howson, who took a touch to steady himself on the edge of the box, then swung his left boot at the ball. 'But hang on a minute, here's Howson, can he win it? YES. HE. CAN! LEEDS UNITED ARE ON THEIR WAY TO WEMBLEY!'

> *Jonny Howson: 'I was confident with my left foot and my initial thought was to curl it into the top-left corner, but for whatever reason I changed my mind and went for the other corner. Let's be honest, I didn't hit it too cleanly, and it bobbled up over the defender's foot and just out the reach of Keiren Westwood. He'd made some top saves, especially in the first leg, and the one you don't hit too cleanly is the one that beats him!'*

The ball seemed to travel in slow motion on its way into the net, and when it finally nestled I couldn't believe my eyes. In the list of my greatest highs from 18 years of supporting Leeds United, this moment went straight in at number one. Lee Bowyer's goals against Anderlecht and AC Milan, Mark Viduka's fourth against Liverpool, Carl Shutt's late winner at the Camp Nou, they all made way for a goal scored at Brunton Park on a Thursday night, in front of fewer than 13,000 fans, in the third tier of English football.

> *David Prutton: 'It was an amazing night. We knew we had the quality to get ourselves back in the game, but we needed someone to step up, and Jonny Howson was the perfect kid to get the goals that took us to Wembley.'*

I'd pay serious money to see five minutes of CCTV footage from the moment Howson scored. The pub went absolutely bonkers, and after a few seconds of 'calm' during the final seconds of play, the pub went absolutely bonkers again when the final whistle blew. What a sight it must have been for the bar staff, and what a job they had on their hands to clear the millions of shards of glass that covered the floor of the entire pub. The only footage that I'm aware of was captured by my friend Terry, who filmed the pub singing 'Marching On Together' in the aftermath. It's quite the watch and the sort of euphoric scenes that only a football fan can experience, proving that it really doesn't matter what level you are competing at. Football is about emotions not status, and this had been an emotional roller coaster of a season like few others, even by Leeds United's standards.

> *Jonny Howson: 'To score the two goals to take us to Wembley – even more so a last-minute one – the emotion, it was just unbelievable. You look back on your career, and the sacrifices you've had to make and the hard work you've had to go through to get in the position to be a professional footballer, it's all for moments like that. I'm not ashamed of the amount I've watched that goal back. And I don't judge it as a football moment, it was a life moment.'*

Doncaster Rovers 1 Leeds United 0

Play-off final
Wembley (75,132)

> *'The highlight of your career when you lose 1-0 in the play-off final!' – Casper Ankergren*

Leeds United were going to Wembley. I'd yearned for this for years. I missed the chance to go in 1996 – when Gary McAllister was captain and Leeds were stuffed 3-0 in the

League Cup Final by Aston Villa – and 'getting to Wembley' had been beyond the club ever since. We had finally made it, but with Leeds there's always a catch, and the old Wembley, the real Wembley, was gone forever. 'Getting to Wembley' now meant visiting a generic new stadium built on the site of the treacherous felling of the Twin Towers, to face Doncaster Rovers in the League One play-off final.

With a huge allocation of 45,000, season ticket holders were allowed to purchase three extra tickets, which resulted in people sleeping outside the ticket office on the night before they went on sale, to make sure they could buy for their mates too. I was a bit more relaxed about it and headed down to Elland Road after opening up Chem-Dry HQ at 8.15am. It was a boiling hot day and the queues were long, but by lunchtime I had mine and Paul's full ticket allocation in my hands. We were off to Wembley!

Jonny Howson: 'As young lads, you sometimes don't understand how big it actually is. When you're young you have no fear, you just go and play, and it was a bit like that. I was a bit nervous because I was dying to win, but I was also excited for the occasion. A lot of people never get the chance to play at Wembley, so to do it as a teenager was something special.'

We had a fair old crew for the big day. I drove down with Paul, Nige and Taylor, while my brother, Gianni, a Liverpool fan who was just coming for the craic, drove down with Lewis and Fan. George and Cowling already lived in London and would meet us at The Globe, a notorious pub for Wembley trips that I'd looked forward to visiting, though it was so busy we ended up drinking tinnies on the packed streets outside, singing and laughing. Only the football could ruin this lovely day.

It was a rueful walk down Wembley Way, staring at that big stupid arch, the best replacement for the Twin Towers the leaders of the beautiful game could come up with. As we walked through the turnstiles and headed for the nearest bar, I couldn't help imagining what it would have been like to be inside the old Wembley rather than this soulless structure with no history, only apathy. However, once we headed to our seats it was impossible not to be impressed at the size of the place, it was huge, and the Leeds fans packed out one half of the ground. In the other half, Doncaster couldn't even pack out the bottom tier. Funnier still, there was a group of a few thousand Leeds fans in their top tier – only Leeds could have an away end in a cup final!

David Prutton: 'Historically, Leeds United and Donny Rovers exist on different football planets, and that was reflected in the huge turnout from our fans. We were a club that had very recently been rubbing shoulders with the best teams in Europe and now was on its knees, slowly staggering to its feet.'

Just as against Watford in the Championship play-off final, a 2-0 away win in the semi-final second leg meant an unchanged and slightly unbalanced team for the final. Alan Sheehan was available again after suspension but McAllister stuck with Bradley Johnson in an unnatural left-back role.

Bradley Johnson: 'The last game of the season against Gillingham was my first time at left-back. I really enjoyed it and the manager fancied me there, but I was surprised when I kept my place after we lost the first leg against Carlisle. Once we were through, McAllister told me he couldn't change a winning team and asked if I could play left-back in the final. "Errrrr, yeah no problem!" I was a bit taken aback, but of course I'd have played anywhere.'

Using Johnson at left-back resulted in an imbalanced midfield too, with Prutton in an unfamiliar role on the left of the diamond and Kilkenny filling in uncomfortably on the right. It wasn't ideal, certainly against a well-drilled and tightly knit opponent. Doncaster had been a non-league team just five years earlier, but manager Sean O'Driscoll had built a solid side that should have claimed automatic promotion. They had overcome that disappointment by thrashing Southend United 5-1 in their semi-final second leg, and they had recent experience of winning a final too, having won the Football League Trophy in the previous season. Both league fixtures had produced tight 1-0 away wins, so the teams were clearly evenly matched and everybody was expecting a tough game, especially Beckford.

Jermaine Beckford: 'I still hadn't recovered from my injury against Carlisle; it was causing me all sorts of problems. My ankle was heavily strapped up and I was pumped up with painkillers, but this was Wembley, I had to play. I just had to. Even if I only got an hour, or 45 minutes, surely there was something I could do: get on the end of something, a little bit of instinctive finishing, or something off the cuff.'

The Leeds fans were in fine voice from the moment the players emerged from the tunnel, and their spirits were raised as Johnson fired a long-range piledriver over the bar within minutes of kick-off. However, Doncaster soon took complete control, with their quick, one-touch passing leaving United chasing shadows. Casper Ankergren needed to be on top of his game to keep Leeds level, thrice rushing out to steal the ball off the toes of Doncaster attackers as red and white hoops cut through his defence almost at will.

The Leeds players looked shellshocked and their Yorkshire rivals' confidence was soaring, but the enthusiasm from the

Whites fans eventually dragged their team back into the game. Beckford had a couple of sniffs at goal as Leeds began to settle, and at the end of a high-octane half Howson found space on the edge of the box but his 20-yard curler sailed inches over the bar.

> *Jonny Howson: 'It was the type of shot I favoured, if only it would have been a few inches lower. I swore in frustration and the camera had just panned to me, and I remember my mum after the game saying, "I can't believe you swore on that big screen!"'*

It was Leeds's best chance of the match and left me with a positive feeling during half-time beers. Having been totally outplayed in the opening stages, McAllister's team had weathered the storm and were starting to take control. It was all to play for in the second half and I was sure Doncaster would tire, that Leeds would get Dougie Freedman on the ball more, that Beckford's pace would cause all sorts of problems, and that this really would be our day, our season, at last.

Fat chance. Two minutes into the second half Doncaster opened the scoring without Leeds even touching the ball (with the exception of two deflections). Many fans were still in the bar and, judging by the marking, the players' heads were still in the dressing room when James Hayter headed home from a corner, a goal that gets worse each time you see it. Hayter's job was to stand on the keeper and be a nuisance, but he drifted out to the penalty spot as the corner was about to be taken. Howson was the first to spot the issue and pointed at Hayter, then captain Jonathan Douglas pointed at him, but nobody did anything. Three defenders were drawn by runs to the near post, the corner floated over them all and landed plumb on the head of Hayter, who was all alone and didn't even need to jump to plant an unstoppable header past Ankergren. Now it was

Johnson's turn to point at Hayter, but it was too late. What a way to start the half.

> *Bradley Johnson: 'People might be surprised, but we didn't do any work on set plays. And to concede a goal from a set play like that, in such a big game, it was schoolboy stuff.'*

Despite the nightmare start, the second half continued in the 'blood-and-thunder' manner of the first. This was not a frozen, insipid performance like Leeds had produced in their previous two finals, but Doncaster were able to repel an attempted onslaught with relative comfort. From three sniffs at goal Beckford couldn't stretch Neil Sullivan, and birthday boy Freedman, 34 on the day and mesmerising in recent weeks, just couldn't get a grip on the game. Even so, it was still mystifying when Freedman was withdrawn for the last 15 minutes, the second of two quickfire substitutions by McAllister that seemed panicky, and proved misguided. Freedman and Prutton had been McAllister's two best players during the run-in, but they were replaced by the industrious Andy Hughes and Trésor Kandol, who had been frozen out for much of the second half of the season. It was a move more suited to the managerial style of Dennis Wise – out went the patience that McAllister's philosophy was built upon, in came Wise's route-one approach.

> *David Prutton: 'Once I was substituted I was going through exactly what the fans were going through, pleading with someone to do something because time was running out.'*

Leeds had scored almost a third of their goals in the last ten minutes of matches in 2007/08 so I remained hopeful, but what worked so often for Wise didn't work for McAllister because every ball into the box was claimed by a goalkeeper who the Whites had released almost a year ago to the day. Sullivan was terrific in the Championship, but Wise felt he was overweight and let Tony Warner and Graham Stack battle it out for his jersey as the Whites sunk to the bottom of the league. 'He felt he was capable of playing in goal for us and I didn't,' remarked Wise before the teams met at Elland Road earlier in the season. Sullivan proved Wise wrong with a virtuoso display at Wembley, his gloves like magnets to the ball, stifling the Whites as they ran out of ideas.

Leeds had scored eight goals in injury time this season, but my hope had turned into hopeless desperation as we entered the dying embers. Paul Green would sign for Leeds a few years later but I never saw him play anything like he did on this afternoon at Wembley; he was everywhere, and in the fifth minute of added time Green's calm header back to Sullivan, under intense pressure, was the moment all hope was gone. The full-time whistle blew and Doncaster had done it. After a 50-year absence they were back in the second tier. Leeds, meanwhile, had done it again. Another play-off final defeat, another Wembley defeat, a whole season's work up in smoke.

Bradley Johnson: 'There haven't been many days when I've cried in football but that was certainly one. I cried my eyes out after the match.'

After the Watford defeat in 2006 I had been furious at Kevin Blackwell for getting his selection and tactics spectacularly wrong from start to finish, but after this defeat I was just gutted; for myself, for the fans, and for the players too. They'd run through brick walls all season and been the second-best team by one point, despite managers and coaches coming and going, team-mates coming and going, not to mention all the administrational and disciplinary distractions off the pitch too.

They had done incredibly well, but they had failed, and Leeds
United would remain a League One club next season …

> *David Prutton: 'It was a bit like that analogy of climbing a
> mountain. You think you've reached the last peak and you're
> about to plant your flag in the ground, then you turn around
> and are like, "Fucking hell, look at that! Where's that come
> from?" That's what that weekend at Wembley was like. One
> part of you is thinking we did well to overcome all those
> obstacles, but the clearer-sighted side knows that we should
> have got promoted.'*

'It looks as though we'll have to try and win it again,' were the
words Gary McAllister heard his manager say after Leeds
won the title in 1992, and 16 years later, as boss of the club
himself, he echoed Howard Wilkinson's sentiment, 'In real
terms, the players earned 91 points which would have won
promotion comfortably, but the challenge is now to repeat
it.' The challenge wasn't a small one. Leeds were relegated to
League One the season after losing their last play-off final,
and United's man of the match at Wembley summed up the
players' disappointment, and the magnitude of the task to pick
themselves up.

> *Casper Ankergren: 'It was a really emotional day. You're
> happy with your performance but you can do nothing with
> it, you didn't achieve what you wanted to achieve. I ended
> up taking myself away from the lads after the game, crying
> because I was so disappointed not to win. It took me quite a
> while to get over that.'*

League One table 2007/08

	P	W	D	L	F	A	Pts
Swansea	46	27	11	8	82	42	92
Nottingham Forest	46	22	16	8	64	32	82
Doncaster Rovers (P)	46	23	11	12	65	41	80
Carlisle United	46	23	11	12	64	46	80
LEEDS UNITED*	**46**	**27**	**10**	**9**	**72**	**38**	**76**
Southend United	46	22	10	14	70	55	76
Brighton & Hove Albion	46	19	12	15	58	50	69
Oldham Athletic	46	18	13	15	58	46	67
Northampton Town	46	17	15	14	60	55	66
Huddersfield Town	46	20	6	20	50	62	66
Tranmere Rovers	46	18	11	17	52	47	65
Walsall	46	16	16	14	52	46	64
Swindon Town	46	16	13	17	63	56	61
Leyton Orient	46	16	12	18	49	63	60
Hartlepool United	46	15	9	22	63	66	54
Bristol Rovers	46	12	17	17	45	53	53
Millwall	46	14	10	22	45	60	52
Yeovil Town	46	14	10	22	38	59	52
Cheltenham Town	46	13	12	21	42	64	51
Crewe Alexandra	46	12	14	20	47	65	50
Bournemouth**	46	17	7	22	62	72	48
Gillingham	46	11	13	22	44	73	46
Port Vale	46	9	11	26	47	81	38
Luton Town***	46	11	10	25	43	63	33

*Leeds deducted 15 points
**Bournemouth deducted 10 points
***Luton deducted 10 points

PART TWO: 2008/09

SECOND SEASON SYNDROME

INTRODUCTION

By Jermaine Beckford

It just wasn't to be at Wembley, and that was really tough because we all believed we had enough in the dressing room. And we did, we had more than enough, but it just wasn't our day. Knowing what it had taken to get to that point, then adding in all the hype, all the energy, all the excitement around us, and the electric atmosphere from our fans at Wembley, only to go out and lose 1-0 – it was by far the lowest point of my career. By far. We had a few weeks to get our minds and our heads together, to dust ourselves off, and a few of the boys went on holiday together to draw a line under that chapter and start again afresh.

Before the first training session of pre-season we spoke about the crazy odds we'd overcome to get to the play-off final at Wembley. We had a 15-point deduction – we were adrift at sea – and we had injuries, suspensions, managerial changes and all the other externals, but we managed to overcome absolutely everything to get to that point where we were playing in the play-off final. So, imagine what we could achieve without those obstacles in our way? We were convinced we would bounce back, hit the right strides and achieve promotion. We truly believed we would do it.

Leeds United 4 FCV Dender 1

Pre-season friendly
Elland Road (7,041)

> 'Delphy started pre-season with us and he was unbelievable,
> he was unreal. I'd never seen a young player as good as him.'
> – Bradley Johnson

Ken Bates couldn't seem to go any stretch of time without antagonising the Leeds fans. Within weeks of arriving at the club he had hiked the ticket prices, removed the option to pay for season tickets in instalments, and forced season ticket holders to cough up the full amount before the season had ended, or pay an even more inflated price for a 'late' renewal. A true snollygoster, Bates sank to cartoonish levels of villainy when he kicked families out of the central areas in the East Stand because those seats had the best view, for which he could charge a premium.

Another source of aggravation was the impression our money was being used to fund a never-ending run of legal battles that Bates became embroiled in, and his constant war of words with Leeds City Council, the *Yorkshire Evening Post*, and anybody who dared question his leadership was tiresome in the extreme. Bates's latest trick was to strip Radio Leeds of their commentary rights after 40 years covering the club. Instead, the rights were awarded to Bates's own in-house digital station, Yorkshire Radio. More nonsensical propaganda was coming our way in 2008/09.

Gary McAllister's revolution gathered pace over the summer. He had transformed the style of the team and now he needed to offload the dead wood from the previous season's enforced scattergun approach to recruitment. Considering Leeds had used a whopping 39 players in 2007/08, it was quite the job. Seb Carole, Matt Heath, Alan Thompson, Leon

Constantine, Ian Westlake, Curtis Weston, Filipe da Costa, Darren Kenton, Anthony Elding and Sebastian Sorsa were all successfully disposed of (the latter having failed to make a single appearance), but Peter Sweeney and Ian Westlake were unable to find new clubs and consigned to the reserves. Trésor Kandol also didn't feature in McAllister's plans, but his Leeds career was given a stay of execution as he headed to Millwall on loan.

In terms of incomings, McAllister's priority was improving the team at the top end of the pitch and he couldn't have made a faster start. Leeds's first signing of the summer was made in the hours before the play-off final, and it was a real statement of intent. Swansea's Scouse winger Andy Robinson, who had been instrumental in helping his team to the League One title, had rejected a new contract at the Liberty Stadium and signed for Leeds instead. Robinson didn't care what division he would be playing in as long as it was for Leeds, which was great to hear, and I couldn't wait to see him strutting his stuff at Elland Road. McAllister headed north of the border to fill the vacancy on the other flank, spending a nominal five-figure sum on Livingston's 20-year-old winger Robert Snodgrass. Snoddy's claim to fame was turning down a move to Barcelona as a teenager, and Leeds had high hopes that he could make an instant impact in League One. Enoch Showunmi was a like-for-like replacement for Kandol, but the most difficult task of the summer was always going to be replacing Dougie Freedman, who had been so instrumental in the run-in. Enter the stage, Luciano Becchio.

Just the name was a turn-on, as was the fact that Becchio was an Argentinian former Barcelona B striker (in a parallel universe Becchio and Snodgrass could have been tearing it up at Barca's famous La Masia academy). Becchio joined the pre-season tour of Ireland as a trialist, but soon signed a permanent deal for around £300,000 from Spanish third-tier side Mérida.

Luciano Becchio: 'I had three offers from second-division clubs in Spain, but I decided to test myself with Leeds, a great club that was going through a bad situation.'

McAllister's business was complete, but not his elevation of the quality in the squad, for Leeds had a teenage sensation in the reserves who was promoted to the first team for the 2008/09 season. Fabian Delph was so good that Leeds had tried to keep his talent under wraps – they were sure he was the next star to emerge from the Thorp Arch academy. The first time I set eyes on him I could see why. It was during the season's curtain-raiser at home to Belgian top-division side, FCV Dender, in front of an Elland Road crowd that was so sparse Paul and I could sit down, drape our legs over the seats in front and relax. Paul was living his dream. We would have been on the edge of our seats but for the devastating news that Becchio had picked up a minor knock and wouldn't feature, although when Delph came on our eyes were popping out of our heads.

He was introduced with half an hour to go and instantly stood out a mile. A small, wiry midfielder, with a burst of pace and the ball tied to his shoelaces, Delph also had a box of tricks and dipped into it a couple of times during an extraordinary cameo, running rings around the opponents. We had another gem in our ranks. Leeds ran out comfortable 4-1 winners but I can't remember any of the goals, the only thing imprinted on my mind that day was the performance of Delph, and it really got the juices flowing for the season to come.

'People say we're a big club, but let's be realistic. All we are at the moment is a well supported team in the third division.' McAllister's words weren't meant to dampen expectation, they were to instil the attitude that no football club has a God-given right to do anything. The players would have to earn promotion on the pitch, and this time there could be no excuses.

Scunthorpe United 1 Leeds United 2

Matchday 1 of 46
Glanford Park (8,315)

> *'If we wouldn't have had the minus 15 we'd have been*
> *promoted fairly easily, so we probably just expected to go on*
> *and get automatic promotion without any trouble. But you*
> *soon realise football doesn't work like that.' – Jonny Howson*

The League One season kicked off at high noon in sunny
Scunny. The game wasn't televised, just brought forward on
police advice, and the day got off to a bad start when I was
flashed by a speed camera heading down the M180. North
Yorkshiremen are blessed to live in the only county in England
without speed cameras, but once we cross the borders it
becomes a curse as we aren't used to looking out for them. My
driving licence clocked up its first three points of the season
and I was expecting the same for Leeds, but this would not
be an easy game. Scunthorpe were freshly relegated from
the Championship and had retained their star striker, Gary
Hooper, for their battle to bounce back at the first attempt.

I had never been to Glanford Park, and from the outside
the corrugated iron structure made it look less like a football
stadium and more like the Chem-Dry unit (just a lot smaller),
but once inside it possessed a lot more charm. It was tight and
compact, a great little ground to visit, and Leeds were allocated
the stand behind the goal and a section down the touchline
too, which is where Paul and I were stood.

McAllister's first line-up of the season would be telling,
and having concentrated on bolstering his attacking options
it was no surprise to see Leeds employing a more regular
4-4-2 rather than the diamond midfield of the previous
season. Four of the summer signings started the game, but
Luciano Becchio had to settle for a place on the bench as

Enoch Showunmi got the nod to partner Beckford up front. Andy Robinson and Robert Snodgrass patrolled the wings, ably backed up by attacking full-backs, Alan Sheehan (who had now signed on permanently from Leicester) and Frazer Richardson, the new club captain. Having been stripped of the captaincy, Jonathan Douglas was also stripped of his place in the team, with Prutton and Howson preferred in the engine room.

'Paper teams win paper cups' was a famous quote from the great Howard Wilkinson, and although Leeds's midfield looked great on paper it just wasn't clicking in the flesh – Prutton and Howson were both used to playing alongside a holding midfielder and were completely overrun.

> *David Prutton: 'With the energy Jonny had, he was always the one bombing up and down, so I'm not sure what that left me to do. I was never going to be a "number four", sat at the base of midfield spraying passes!'*

It would have been a relief to reach half-time on level terms, but when the whistle blew the players were incredulous. With the last attack Snodgrass's shot had been fumbled over the line by the goalkeeper, yet the linesman failed to award the goal. Without being able to judge from the opposite end of the ground, the Leeds fans were furious by association.

Our fury was amplified ten minutes after the restart when Hooper edged Scunthorpe ahead, though the delight of the home fans was short-lived as Snodgrass's beautiful free kick was headed home by fellow debutant Showunmi. Paul laughed as I proclaimed Snodgrass's delivery was 'world-class', but I was serious! Whether at the local park or at Wembley, a flat cross whipped in at pace like Snoddy's at Scunny is still a top-level skill. With their tails up Leeds began to take control, and after having a goal ruled out for offside, Beckford got on the scoresheet with ten minutes remaining, pouncing on a rebound after Prutton's shot from a clever short corner had crashed off the bar. The away fans went crazy, and it was great to get a full view of the stand behind the goal, limbs flying everywhere as the players celebrated by the corner flag in front of us.

There was more excitement immediately after the goal, when into the fray came Becchio. When you think 'Argentinian number ten' you immediately think of Diego Maradona, but with his long blond hair controlled by an Alice band, Becchio could only be likened to Claudio Caniggia. He looked a star, and a star was born with his first contribution. Picking up the ball midway into the Scunthorpe half, Becchio had the space to turn and fire a thunderous long-range effort towards goal, beating the keeper all ends up only to be denied by the crossbar. Me and Paul looked at each other open-mouthed; our expectations of Becchio had been ramped up five-fold. Behind the scenes the Argentine had settled quickly and found a home from home in Yorkshire, and Beckford was teaching him the English language and English sense of humour all at the same time.

Jermaine Beckford: 'He didn't speak very good English so I decided to teach him the lingo, the correct phrases and all that stuff. I remember we went to a restaurant and I told him how to thank the waiter and ask for more. When the waiter came over Luciano did as instructed, "This food is shit, can I please have different?" The waiter was shocked of course, asking, "You don't like it?" and Luciano says, "Yes, yes, this food is shit!" But don't worry, he got me back when I asked him to teach me Spanish!'

With a 2-1 victory Leeds were up and running, straight to the top of League One if only for a couple hours, with a points tally of plus three. Next up was a League Cup tie at Chester City, broadcast live on Sky. The country was treated to an irresistible first-half display by Leeds, who raced into a 5-1 half-time lead thanks to Beckford's hat-trick, the best treble scored by a Leeds player in my lifetime. For the first goal Beckford lunged to divert Ankergren's long free kick into the bottom corner with a flick of his toe, a remarkable finish when seen from the right angle. For the second Beckford pounced on a defender's heavy touch and rifled an unstoppable 25-yard left-footed drive into the top corner, and the hat-trick goal was the best of the lot, a majestic right-footed chip that floated divinely into the same top corner.

My excitement was significantly amplified by the fact I had placed a £5 bet on Beckford to score a hat-trick and Leeds to win, as a double, at odds of 30/1. Online betting was still in its infancy; instead we would go into 'betting shops', and I wasn't sure the human at the till would accept my bet so asked for clarification that the double was legitimate. The man confirmed that it was OK and took the bet and my money. I was watching the game with Paul and Rick at Burke Street, and I was so exhilarated that I set off to collect my winnings at half-time, before Rick reminded me that Beckford may have scored a hat-trick but Leeds hadn't won yet, even if they were 5-1 up.

Sadly, the story doesn't end there. When I triumphantly marched to the bookies after the 5-2 victory, they informed me that my bet was invalid because you can't do a double on two incidents that directly affect each other (if Beckford scores a hat-trick, Leeds's odds of winning would drastically shorten). I was outraged, and calmly explained that I had checked with the clerk that the bet was acceptable, and that a betting slip is a binding agreement. Still they wouldn't cough up, but after a couple of phone calls they finally agreed to pay me out, although only on the hat-trick.

Leeds United 5 Crewe Alexandra 2

Matchday 5 of 46
Elland Road (20,075)

> 'There was a very big difference with Delph, even compared to the young players I saw at Barcelona. It was his intensity, which for me is the most important thing. Fab bit you, he put a lot of pressure on you. I loved how he played.' – Luciano Becchio

After a shock 2-0 defeat to Oldham in the opening home game of the season, and a frustrating 1-1 draw at Yeovil, Leeds bounced back to form in the League Cup second round. I was one of only 10,000 in attendance at Elland Road as McAllister's team turned in a virtuoso performance, thrashing Crystal Palace of the Championship 4-0. Low attendances were always given a free pass when it came to the cups, the diehard supporters accepting that only the league really mattered, and low cup attendances were a source of pride for the hardy folks who turned up. However, when a league attendance fell below 25,000 it would always bring derision from the terraces, and with the novelty of League One wearing off and patience with Ken Bates wearing thin, large areas of Elland Road were consistently left desolate.

The Kop was always full, no matter the opponents or competition, but the South Stand was often left empty, the ridiculously expensive wooden seats in the decrepit West Stand were always sparse, and thanks to Bates shunting families from the halfway line out to the corner flags, the East Stand was populated by three unsightly chunks of people: the north end families, the south end families, and the rich scabs in the middle who had stolen the nice seats from the poor children. The East Stand's upper tier wasn't even open for business, ever since Bates realised he could save a few pennies in business rates by keeping it closed. Bates had hoped McAllister's attractive football would keep the fans onside despite another season in the third tier, but Yorkshiremen like value for money and only the hardcore were going to pay Premier League prices for League One football.

The next game brought another poor crowd of just 21,000, and another poor result, 2-2 against Bristol Rovers. With five points from the opening four matches it had been a stuttering start. United were playing some lovely free-flowing attacking football but a leaky defence was costing them dear. For the visit of Crewe Alexandra there was a new centre-back partnership on show, with injuries ruling out both Rui Marques and Paul Huntington. In the short term some people may have felt these injuries were a blessing, but in the case of Huntington the consequences were dire. He had captained the side during pre-season but less than two months later, two weeks before his 21st birthday, a season that had promised so much was over, and so too was Huntington's Leeds career. After a succession of injuries he never played for the club again.

The new centre-back pairing was Ľubomír Michalík and a surprise late addition to the squad, 36-year-old Paul Telfer. The surprise wasn't just down to Telfer's age, or his lack of pace and height. The former Coventry man had retired 18 months earlier, and after an unsuccessful comeback attempt, he had retired again in December of the previous season. But after training with Leeds over the summer McAllister believed his former team-mate could still do a job, and Telfer agreed to give professional football one more go.

It wasn't just the defence that was all change, McAllister overhauled his midfield too. The quartet that started the season – Prutton, Howson, Robinson and Snodgrass – were all on the bench against Crewe, with Hughes, Douglas and Kilkenny recalled to the side, alongside Fabian Delph, who had taken no time to force his way into the team. Bradley

Johnson was left out of the squad entirely and would soon take the difficult decision to go out on a short-term loan, with first-team opportunities few and far between.

> *Bradley Johnson: 'These things happen in football. Another left-sided midfielder emerged that the manager thought was better than me, and that's fair, I can deal with it – Fab was better than me! I didn't want to sit around and not play so I decided to go out on loan and play games. I was a bit upset but I've always been confident in my own ability. I knew I'd be coming back in January and always believed that I'd get back in the team.'*

The wholesale changes were an indication of Leeds's strength in depth, but it also highlighted the manager's uncertainty about his best team. McAllister couldn't even decide on his best goalkeeper, and on this occasion David Lucas was given the nod ahead of Casper Ankergren, a decision that came as a greater surprise to the fans than it did to the Dane.

> *Casper Ankergren: 'I didn't play well in the first part of the season, I was struggling. Perhaps I hadn't fully recovered from the play-off final defeat. We chopped and changed goalkeepers and it wasn't helpful for anyone, the defence couldn't get settled.'*

The third home game of the season drew yet another distressingly low attendance of barely 20,000, but the crowd were buoyant as Leeds clicked into gear. Delph celebrated signing a new four-year contract with his first professional goal, a long-range effort to open the scoring midway through the first half. Alan Sheehan doubled the lead with a long-range strike of his own, and at half-time Leeds were on course for a comfortable victory. The goal glut continued in the second half with Crewe putting up little resistance. Jonathan Douglas made it 3-0 just after the break, then Beckford grabbed his customary goal before substitute Andy Robinson put the icing on the cake with a lovely curling strike in the closing stages.

Unfortunately, Robinson's goal was not the final action. Two minutes into injury time Michalík soured the victory by getting himself needlessly sent off, and there was still time for not one but two consolation goals for the visitors. It was a frustrating way to end a fantastic performance, and McAllister's defensive woes continued when Sheehan was dismissed ten minutes into the next game at Swindon. Even still, the ten men ground out an impressive 3-1 victory and Leeds were picking up a head of steam.

———

Leeds United 1 Hereford United 0
Matchday 8 of 46
Elland Road (25,676)

> *'It was incredible to feel so much love. I will always have the Leeds fans in my heart.' – Luciano Becchio*

Leeds returned to the scene of their epic play-off semi-final victory and secured a repeat result, 2-0 at Carlisle, this time with little fuss. The clean sheet was their first of the league campaign, and coupled with goals for each of his strikers, McAllister must have been thrilled with a great afternoon's work. Beckford and Becchio looked a match made in heaven, and the Argentine's relationship with Beckford came as naturally as the love he received from the fans, who had instantly bestowed cult hero status upon their Argentinian number ten.

> *Luciano Becchio: 'Becks is a great person, he helped me a lot and we made good friends outside of football. Obviously that*

*helps a lot to understand each other when playing football
together. I have no doubt that the support of the fans helped
in my performances too.'*

*Jermaine Beckford: 'I absolutely loved playing with Luciano,
absolutely loved it. We had a great connection immediately
and built such a great bond, on and off the field. It was
amazing.'*

Leeds had completely recovered from a dodgy opening to
the season. They were up to third in the league, and three
great wins in the League Cup helped build momentum as
the Whites stormed into the last 16, scoring 12 goals in the
process. In all competitions Leeds were on a five-match
winning run and had now won eight of their 11 games. The
feelgood factor was also helped by a lack of background noise
this season, although the club had been charged by the FA
after making payments to unlicensed agents in the transfer
of Anthony Elding. This minor infringement wasn't going
to cause much distraction though; in fact it was thoroughly
refreshing when Ken Bates pleaded guilty to the crime,
resulting in a small £7,000 fine.

The soaring confidence led to Elland Road's largest crowd
of the season for the visit of bottom side Hereford. For this
game Rick took my ticket in the Kop, while I went suited and
booted in the South Stand executive boxes with my brother
Gianni, and brother-in-law Josh. I'm not entirely sure why we
were in an executive box, it must have been something to do
with Chem-Dry somehow, but it was an enjoyable experience
as a one-off. There was cheap plonk on arrival, accompanied by
a fancy team sheet which delivered the most exciting line-up of
the season. Andy Robinson was recalled, and both Delph and
Howson started in midfield, with Jonathan Douglas's presence
giving them the freedom to roam. It was quite the supply line

for a strike force that were on fire, especially Beckford, who had reached 'goal machine' level with 11 in 11 games.

You may have expected Hereford, newly promoted and looking out of their depth at the higher level, to be quaking in their boots, yet they had played Leeds home and away in the 2007/08 FA Cup without conceding a goal, drawing 0-0 before winning an Elland Road replay 1-0, so perhaps this wouldn't quite be the walk in the park everybody expected. Nonetheless, the mood in the not-so-posh executive box was happy and relaxed as we supped cheap beer (slyly, as you aren't allowed to drink alcohol during the match) and grazed on a beige buffet, while waiting patiently for Leeds to go in front. The main drawback of being in an executive box is the Perspex screen that separates you from the action (especially on a beautiful autumn afternoon). It doesn't hinder your view but completely dims the atmosphere, not that there was too much excitement in the stands during a first half in which Hereford repelled all attacks with relative comfort.

As the minutes ticked by the result everybody had expected was cast deeper into doubt. Hereford were defending stubbornly, led by surely one of the most famous players to drop to League One, 37-year-old Bruno N'Gotty, once of AC Milan and France. Their young goalkeeper Darren Randolph was looking unbeatable, but his 72nd-minute save from a Becchio header cruelly landed kindly for Andy Robinson, who couldn't miss. It was the least United deserved, and a sixth victory on the bounce was never in doubt once the deadlock had been broken. A further bonus was another clean sheet for a defence that had been steadied by the presence of Paul Telfer, who was thriving in a team that dominated possession and didn't have too much defending to do. Paul and I joked that it was like having Fabio Cannavaro in defence, who was also greater in stature than in build (interestingly, they both measure 5ft 9in according to Wikipedia).

Gary McAllister praised the Leeds fans after the game, suggesting that in years gone by the crowd would have got frustrated and perhaps become counterproductive. It was a sign that the supporters believed in his team, but that belief was challenged through a difficult October. Leeds started and ended the month in third position, winning all three home games but losing all three on their travels.

The first defeat at Peterborough was digestible, not just because it was only the second defeat of the season but also thanks to Leeds Rhinos retaining their Super League crown by again beating favourites St Helens in the Old Trafford Grand Final. The next defeat at Millwall was harder to take, and by the time United succumbed to defeat at Southend the away form had become a major talking point, especially as there had been a fourth away defeat in the Football League Trophy, 4-2 to Rotherham United at the Don Valley Stadium. It was a pattern of results that was too coincidental not to be taken seriously – the Whites appeared to have a soft underbelly, at least away from the home comforts of Elland Road. McAllister knew as well as anybody that such inconsistent form wouldn't keep his side in the promotion mix for much longer, but a new month brought a buck to the trend and a welcome away victory at Cheltenham lifted Leeds into the automatic promotion places heading into the final international break of the year.

—

Derby County 2 Leeds United 1
League Cup fourth round
Pride Park (18,540)

*'That was the moment when I first thought, "Wow. He is special." I was sat on the bench at the time but you've got to admire it, and as a Leeds fan it was brilliant to watch.' –
Jonny Howson*

It had been ten years since Leeds last played on my birthday, a League Cup fourth round tie at Leicester which is still etched in my memory as one of the most painful defeats of my life. Ten birthdays later and I was heading back to the East Midlands with a quarter-final spot up for grabs once again. I'd supported one of the biggest clubs in the country for over 15 years but only ever seen them progress beyond the League Cup fourth round once, a pitiful record, and as a League One club it was impossible to even think about reaching Wembley (although Bradford City would reach the final as a League Two club just a few years later). So Wembley wasn't the motivation when we travelled to Pride Park, it was simply an excuse for a jolly good birthday knees-up.

My brother Gianni joined me, Paul and Rick for the special occasion, and the Leeds fans were allocated the full stand behind the goal which almost guaranteed a good time, especially when the result was practically inconsequential. Leeds might have had no chance of winning the competition but they were certainly capable of beating Derby, who had been relegated from the Premier League the previous season after winning just one match, and accumulating just 11 points (at the time of writing, still the lowest total in history). Paul Jewell's team had taken their poor form into the Championship and were languishing in the bottom half of the table.

As well as the birthday knees-up, we were also looking forward to watching McAllister's free-flowing football, but most of all we were looking forward to watching Fabian Delph in action. What a player this boy was. As soon as he broke into the team he looked the best player, and his performances in League One had attracted widespread Premier League interest, so much so that his chant was simply, 'FABIAN DELPH, IS NOT FOR SALE!' He was quick, silky, intelligent, hard-working, hard in the tackle, and had already scored some spectacular goals. It's no exaggeration to say he was one of the best midfielders I'd seen play for Leeds, and probably the most exciting youth product. There was no doubt in my mind that Delph would play for England, and he had just received his first under-21 cap, making an eye-catching cameo from the bench with two outrageous pieces of skill. For an 18-year-old with only a couple of months' experience playing in League One, representing his country at this level was a superb achievement.

On my 15th birthday at Filbert Street Leeds had dominated the whole match but suffered a nightmare end, conceding two late goals to lose 2-1. On my 25th birthday at Pride Park Leeds dominated the whole match but suffered a nightmare start, conceding two early goals that eventually earned a repeat result. The ease with which Derby cut through the Leeds defence had me bracing myself for an uncomfortable and potentially embarrassing night, but perhaps this lulled the home side into a false sense of security and once they'd taken their foot off the gas they couldn't reassert their authority. After persistent pressure the visitors got their reward in the 40th minute when Luciano Becchio pulled a goal back with a bullet header. It was now six goals in seven games for a striker who was already pulling up trees before hitting his red-hot scoring streak.

In the second half Leeds laid siege to Derby's goal in search of the equaliser, roared on by 3,500 electrified away fans, and led by a teenage rookie. I had been especially keen for my brother to see just how exciting a talent Delph was, and he lived up to his billing with a sensational performance, running rings around the opposition as if he was playing against kids half his age, not seasoned ex-Premier League professionals.

Jonny Howson: 'Robbie Savage was at the back end of his career, but he was still a top player having played so many years in the Premier League [by then at Derby, his previous 11 seasons had been in the Premier League], but he couldn't

get near Delph, he would just drop his shoulder and he'd be
gone. I remember in the end Savage went steaming in to do
him, but Fab just rode it!'

Robert Snodgrass came closest to equalising with a 25-yard free kick that curled fractionally too much and hit the post, though the most notable effort was an exceptional long-range Beckford lob that was inches from catching out the back-pedalling Roy Carroll in the Derby goal.

At the final whistle our fallen heroes took the adulation of the Leeds fans, and both managers too. 'Give Leeds credit, they battered us for 70 minutes,' said a relieved Jewell, while McAllister's sentiment echoed the words spoken by David O'Leary a decade earlier, 'I'm lost for words really. It is a cruel game at times.'

———

Leeds United 1 Huddersfield Town 2
Matchday 16 of 46
Elland Road (32,028)

'It was a derby like the Clásicos in Argentina. In both
countries the supporters are very passionate and encourage
their team until they are speechless.' – Luciano Becchio

The West Yorkshire derby's early kick-off presented Leeds with a chance to top League One for the third time in the club's history, if only for a couple of hours, as they had on the previous two occasions. It was a golden chance too, their opponents were beleaguered and managerless, languishing in 16th position and hadn't won at Elland Road since I was six weeks old. In front of a near capacity crowd (with the east upper closed), few expected that the barren run would end this time, not even me, who nearly always found reasons why Leeds would lose. Even my Huddersfield-supporting friends, Billy and Edwin, were expecting the worst, but for their players it was a chance to make history, to light up their season whatever was to come. A bit like a cup final.

Two of my most hated clichés in football are the overused (even by cliché standards) 'cup final' comparison, and the nonsensical 'scoring too early' theory, but both were unquestionably in play here. Leeds got off to a blistering start, taking the lead when Snodgrass converted from Becchio's cross, right in front of the Huddersfield fans. Only three minutes were on the clock, but rather than pushing home their advantage the Whites slipped into cruise control and soon lost a grip on the match. It was a relief to reach half-time still a goal to the good.

Gary McAllister had picked the same 11 and bench as at Derby, and if their legs were feeling weary from their midweek excursions they would have turned to lead when Huddersfield equalised just 27 seconds into the second half. What a moment it must have been for 19-year-old Huddersfield-born left-back Joe Skarz, his first goal in professional football on his 50th start. Rather than provoking a response from Leeds, the home team stuttered. On came Jermaine Beckford (he had been nursing an injury) but with 15 minutes to go Delph had run his race and without him Leeds totally lost their way.

In the years since losing our Premier League status, the 'UNITED REJECT!' chant, aimed at almost every former Leeds player, had developed into 'YOU'RE TOO SHIT TO PLAY FOR LEEDS!', and Danny Cadamarteri got the full treatment when he came off the bench for the last ten minutes. Cadamarteri only made one appearance for Leeds, and was sold only one month after signing, but typically he was to get the last laugh. I was preparing to settle for a disappointing point when Cadamarteri collected the ball on the right wing a minute into stoppage time, but my heart was in my mouth when he skipped past Paul Telfer and crossed for Michael Collins, whose finish wrong-footed Ankergren and bobbled into the net – a famous winning goal in front of the jubilant Huddersfield fans.

I must admit, the sight of opposing fans celebrating wildly is something I am fascinated by. It's not a 'guilty pleasure', but it sure is a sight to behold and the Terriers milked the moment for all it was worth. 'They'll be dancing in the streets of Cleckheaton, Kirklees, and Birstall tonight,' roared the commentator as we listened in disbelief to the reaction on Radio Leeds (now a Huddersfield channel, after Bates stole the Leeds commentary for Yorkshire Radio). I couldn't speak on the journey home, worse still, we then had to sit through *Soccer Saturday* as our rivals all won, knocking Leeds down to sixth place.

Just two days later they bounced back in style. Beckford was back in the side and bagged his second hat-trick of the season in a 5-2 victory in the FA Cup first round at Northampton Town. Beckford bagged another brace the following Saturday as Hartlepool United were dispatched 4-1 at Elland Road, but eight days after trouncing Northampton in the cup, Leeds returned to the Sixfields for a league fixture and lost 2-1. Beckford scored his sixth goal in three games to draw Leeds level but United capitulated in now typical fashion, conceding an 87th-minute winner that condemned them to a fourth defeat in their last five League One away games. A wretched day for McAllister turned into his worst nightmare when it was confirmed that his team hadn't just lost the match, they'd also lost Beckford to a pulled hamstring.

Jermaine Beckford: 'I was ruled out for six weeks and there wasn't even any international fixtures to buy me some time, I'd be missing around ten games. When you're as hungry and as driven as I was you just want to play every minute of every game, to score goals and win games, so that was really tough to take.'

With his team's confidence draining, Beckford's injury was the last thing McAllister needed, and next up was a trip to a place no Leeds fan had ever heard of to play a team no Leeds fan would ever forget.

Histon 1 Leeds United 0

FA Cup second round
Bridge Road (4,301)

'Errrm … It wasn't a great day, was it!' – Jonny Howson

Leeds's record in the FA Cup was as bad as their abysmal League Cup record. In my time supporting the club three quarter-final defeats (without scoring) were as good as it got, and Leeds hadn't won an FA Cup match for five years before they overcame Northampton in the last round. There had been some embarrassing defeats along the way, although Leeds had never stooped quite so low as losing to a non-league team, in their entire history.

Bridge Road is a tiny stadium in a small Cambridgeshire village. In fact, Histon is such a small village that it entwined with its neighbouring village to become known as Histon and Impington. Its football club is actually older than Leeds United, but that only adds weight to the gulf between the sides. For 90 years Histon competed at county and regional levels, but in the mid-1990s a spate of promotions resulted in them reaching the Conference in 2007, the fifth tier of English football and one level below League Two. Despite taking the decision to remain a part-time club, Histon were riding the crest of a wave and sat proudly on top of the Conference, with the chance to reach the third round for the first time in their history, in only their fourth appearance in the competition's 'proper' rounds. Histon's 104-year history had led them to this moment, a match against the famous Leeds United. The fortunes of the clubs had peaked and plunged at the same moment in time, the draw brought them together, and the magic of the FA Cup did the rest.

It was a Sunday lunchtime kick-off and the rain was lashing down, so much so that the camera lenses were all covered in rain and, ludicrously, seldom wiped. Thus, we spent almost the whole game peering through rain drops. 'Like watching through a fish pond,' observed Ken Bates afterwards. In the 38th minute Histon's captain, Matt Langston, who could be described as a burly postman without any artistic licence in play, rose to head home a corner and put Leeds in a world of trouble. Gary McAllister's job was probably in trouble too. He had picked his strongest team in order to gain some much-needed confidence on the road, minus the injured Beckford of course, and without their prolific striker Leeds were not the same team. It was left to Ľubomír Michalík to try and spare their blushes, but the Slovakian international was denied by the post and a goal-line clearance, and Leeds pulled off the unthinkable and lost to Histon.

> David Prutton: 'I wasn't happy when Gary told me I wouldn't be playing at Histon, but as you're watching it unfold from the bench, aware that history is being made, I couldn't help thinking, "Thank heavens I've been dropped for this!" It was a very quiet dressing room afterwards.'

It was the most embarrassing defeat this 'once proud club' had ever suffered, and questions about McAllister's job were raised immediately. Yet McAllister's boss seemed to take the defeat on the chin. 'The fact of the matter is that we were knocked out, and that's the end of it,' said Bates, before adding a comment that must have unnerved the manager: 'We cannot expect the opposition to stand back in awe to admire our magnificent football skills, we have to match physical presence with physical presence.' McAllister remained stoic about his philosophy and was adamant his team would get through this difficult period, 'I see these boys all week and I know what they are capable of – and we will stick to our footballing principles.'

> *Jonny Howson: 'The disappointments were just building up. Getting relegated to League One, then we had little bits of hope like getting to Wembley, but moments like Histon just knock you right down again. It's tough being part of Leeds United sometimes, and that was a dark day for the club.'*

After beating Leeds, Histon gave Swansea City a fright in round three, eventually succumbing 2-1 at Bridge Road. They also succumbed in the promotion race but a top-half finish in the Conference was still a commendable feat for such a tiny club. Histon dropped like a stone thereafter, suffering four relegations in five seasons, and at the time of writing they compete at the same level as the likes of Tadcaster Albion, Brighouse Town, Pontefract Collieries and Yorkshire Amateurs, but they will always have their day in the sun (or rain).

'We all had work the next day, so we couldn't go too crazy,' said midfielder and car factory worker Nathaniel Knight-Percival, when reminiscing about the match ten years on. But the words of manager Steve Fallon best portrayed just how low Leeds United had sunk, 'It was a huge day for the whole village.'

—

Leeds United 1 Colchester United 2
Matchday 20 of 46
Elland Road (19,625)

'Football is sometimes hard to understand. McAllister was a great person and we were doing a very good job with him, but somehow we entered into a bad dynamic.' – Luciano Becchio

Leeds had stooped to new lows, but the situation was not unrecoverable. Being seventh in the league was well below expectations, although the table was so tight that a couple of wins would catapult Leeds back into the title race. I was hopeful that the Histon debacle would be the kick up the arse the team needed to wake them from their slumber, yet concerns were growing about whether McAllister's men had the fortitude required to mount a serious push for automatic promotion, which was the minimum expectation of the board and fans. The doubts intensified when United clocked up their eighth defeat in ten away games by losing the next match 2-1 at Tranmere Rovers.

Jonny Howson: 'I think the whole club expected promotion. The players, as individuals, right through to the fans, and rightly so with the squad that we had in League One. But that's what can happen when you're not fully at it. You get what you deserve a lot of the time in football.'

It wasn't all doom and gloom at Elland Road though. Cuddly Ken would be enjoying an extra fat turkey this Christmas after the club announced a profit of £4.5m for the 2007/08 season. It was a galling amount of money to make after the same regime wrote off millions of pounds of debt a year earlier, and I can't imagine how those small business which lost thousands of pounds must have felt. Good news for the Leeds fans though? Not really. The £4.5m profit wasn't just a slap in the face of the creditors, but also the supporters. Surely this money could have been spent building a better team than the one which was sliding down the League One table and losing to villages in the FA Cup. The chairman was failing in his responsibility to improve the football team but his own coffers were filling up nicely.

It can't have been a coincidence that Bates chose this moment to reveal the full nature of his Elland Road redevelopment plans, in his programme notes for the Colchester match. Did Bates just want to pull the wool over the eyes of the fans, or did he really want to build new corporate facilities, a hotel, an office block, shops, bars, restaurants, and even a nightclub for all the party people who wished to flock to Beeston on a Saturday night? 'Football stadiums are used for 25 days a year to play football,' said Bates. 'It's important not to forget about the other 340 days you don't play football.' It was a statement that baffled the supporters, who only cared about the 25 footballing days. Preparing the club for challenging the elite while languishing in the lower reaches of the Football League seemed like backwards thinking to them.

Furthermore, it seemed strange that Bates would want to spend money improving a stadium he didn't even own, although the chairman insisted that purchasing the stadium and training ground within the next 12 months was a priority. I wasn't holding my breath. Just in case that wasn't enough to appease the fans, Bates used the strong financial position of the club to deliver a quote that the disgruntled supporters should have had printed on a banner to display at every game in future, 'Leeds is not a selling club nor a feeder club to the Premier League. So long as the fans continue to support Leeds United no good player will leave Elland Road.'

McAllister must have expected a big response against Colchester, who were only two points clear of the relegation zone. I did, too – surely this team was too good to keep losing? There was still no Jermaine Beckford, but there was Becchio, Snodgrass, Delph, Prutton and Kilkenny, with Jonny Howson on the bench for goodness sake! I anticipated a resounding victory that would send a statement to our supporters and our rivals, especially after Robert Snodgrass opened the scoring with a beautifully taken goal, weaving through two defenders and calmly beating the keeper. The young Scotsman's form was a shining light in a difficult season.

Jonny Howson: 'Snods had so much quality on the ball. He could go past players with ease but he didn't have real pace, but that just showed how much ability he had. He had the other side too, he'd get angry and upset and didn't mind letting you know about it, because he cared and was passionate.'

The opening goal proved to be a false dawn. It had been a jittery start from the home side and the goal should have been the perfect tonic, but Leeds continued to look a shadow of the side whose intricate flowing football in the autumn led pundits to compare them to Premier League teams. Things started to go really wrong when the referee incorrectly awarded Colchester a corner in first-half injury time. The Kop's fury at the decision was compounded by the fear that corners brought, or should I say, the horrors that corners brought. Leeds had been conceding from corners every game for weeks, and Dean Hammond was duly left totally unmarked to head past David Lucas. Elland Road was a wet and miserable place through half-time, and things became critical 20 minutes into the second half when David Prutton was sent off for a second bookable offence.

David Prutton: 'The sad thing is, I had that many red cards that it's hard to remember some of them. Some of them were quite low-key!'

It never rains but it pours, and the resulting free kick was expertly curled into the top corner of the South Stand net. The Kop was too despondent to react angrily, but McAllister did, throwing on recent signing Malcolm Christie along with Enoch Showunmi to form a three-pronged attack with Becchio. But there was no coming back for the ten men, who never threatened to penetrate a team that was well organised and finding their feet under their new manager, Paul Lambert.

A mini crisis had become a full-blown crisis and I was left shell-shocked by how badly this season was turning out. A fourth straight defeat was a dangerous way to head into the Chem-Dry Christmas do, and coupled with Rick's attendance (who qualified due to a few weeks' part-time work between jobs) it was a perfect storm. We headed straight to Wetherspoons after the game, and bypassed the pints, straight on to the gin and milks. No surprise then that we were drunk by the time we reached the venue, and by the morning I was overcome by that fiendish blend of wondering what the hell had happened and not wanting to know the answer.

Milton Keynes Dons 3 Leeds United 1
Matchday 21 of 46
Stadium:MK (17,073)

'Before it's even happened you're thinking, "Oh no!"' – *Casper Ankergren*

It must have been tough for the players to show their faces at Thorp Arch on the Monday after the Colchester defeat, and I knew how they felt as I opened up Chem-Dry HQ. At least myself and the players were there to face the music, unlike McAllister's left-hand man, Neil McDonald, who left to become Sam Allardyce's right-hand man at Blackburn. Was he a rat leaving a sinking ship?

McAllister's job was now on the line and his attempts to reinvigorate an ailing squad led to the signing of a new defender called Mansour Assoumani, a French free agent who went straight into the team for the trip to MK Dons. When I heard the team news while looking for a parking spot in Milton Keynes, I predicted to Paul and Rick that it would be Assoumani's only Leeds appearance. I don't mention the hundreds of incorrect predictions I made, but this was one of the good ones.

It was Leeds's first trip to Milton Keynes, to face a ruthlessly ambitious club who had stolen Wimbledon's place in the Football League through very murky means. They had a brand-new, lavish stadium, and Roberto Di Matteo at the helm, a manager who would win the Champions League within four years (not with the Dons). They also had a very good team, whose form was in stark contrast to Leeds. With eight wins from their last nine matches the hosts started the day eight points ahead of the visitors and looked a decent bet to secure back-to-back promotions. Leeds took a huge following down the A1, almost 5,000 travelling fans filling the bottom tier behind the goal, and the corners that swept around too. It was an impressive ground to be fair, though surely too large for such a young and unpopular club. Construction wasn't quite complete, the small upper tier that circled the stadium was built but had no seats, although I'd have preferred bare concrete to the ridiculous padded seating in the lower tier. It was like being in the cinema and I hoped this wasn't the future.

The away end was in fine voice as always, but there was a slightly toxic undertone bubbling away, waiting to explode if things turned sour. One fan didn't want to wait. The bloke stood behind us was booing every touch Leeds had, until Paul eventually snapped and told him to be quiet, albeit in a more industrial manner. Inevitably, an altercation ensued, with the 'supporter' insisting he had every right to abuse our players having followed the club for 30 years, and as a 20-something-year-old, Paul apparently had no right to question him. 'He can only support them for as long as he's been alive!' was my attempt at reason, but the bloke was just getting angrier and angrier, until his mate finally dragged him off for a beer to calm down. We didn't hang around to find out if this questionable solution worked as sensibly we moved to the other side of the goal.

I do wonder how the angry bloke must have reacted to what happened next. Within 17 minutes Leeds were 2-0 down, with both goals coming from shambolically defended corners. The first was a low, near-post delivery that evaded everyone and somehow ended up in the back of the net. The second corner bounced off Assoumani, was hooked on to his own bar by Becchio, and with four defenders static, Aaron Wilbraham turned the rebound into the net. It really was beyond a joke, and the beleaguered players took the brunt of the fury from the fans behind the goal. Casper Ankergren had been back on bench-warming duties since the West Yorkshire derby defeat, but he was all too aware of the mental block that was causing the constant issues from set pieces.

Casper Ankergren: 'We'd opened a can of worms – whenever there was a corner we were panicking about it. We began to focus on it too much but you have to address it, so it's tricky. It's difficult to change the mindset when you are always fearing the worst.'

Normally, when facing a fifth straight defeat the fury of the fans would be directed squarely in the face of the manager, but McAllister had plenty of sympathisers. This wasn't necessarily because of his historic accomplishments with the club, more because Leeds fans loved to blame Ken Bates for anything

117

they could. Maybe if Bates had allowed him to sign more accomplished centre-backs than double-retiree Paul Telfer, and Assoumani, who had failed to find a club since suffering his second consecutive relegation to the German fourth tier, things wouldn't be quite so bad.

I was desperate for Leeds to turn this game around, and four minutes into the second half Robert Snodgrass smashed home a marvellous volley to instil belief in his team-mates and the away end. It was game on and Leeds had all the momentum; the next goal would be crucial. Any optimism was short-lived, as Aaron Wilbraham headed a superb goal just six minutes later. United had a mountain to climb again. The players kept pushing right to the death, doing all they could to save their manager's job, but without Beckford a comeback was beyond them and they duly fell to a 3-1 defeat. Heading into Christmas Leeds were ninth in League One, five points adrift of the play-off spots, 11 behind the second automatic promotion spot, and 15 away from their next opponents, leaders Leicester City.

The writing was on the wall for McAllister. He tried to play the game in the right way and the supporters could see the potential in his team, but he couldn't seem to eradicate the defensive issues and the abysmal away form. So, it came as no great surprise when Bates wielded the axe the next day, with the news of McAllister's sacking filtering through while I was enjoying the Sunday day sesh at Banyan.

David Prutton: 'When a manager who has believed in you gets the sack there is that sense of collectively letting him down. But I'd like to think I was always honest enough in my approach to football that I could look at myself and say, "I might have been crap, but I always gave him as much as I possibly could, physically and mentally." Gary was one of the finest midfielders Leeds United have ever had, he helped put

> *the club back on the map and is still well received at Elland Road to this day, and always will be.'*

I was disappointed to have lost the only Leeds United-minded leader at the club, but it was hard to argue with the decision. The bookies and the media unanimously agreed that McAllister's replacement would be Bates's old mate, Gus Poyet, who had recently lost his job as assistant manager at Tottenham following the sacking of Juande Ramos. I begrudgingly accepted the inevitable, and I was even coming around to the idea when reports emerged that Bates's number one target was in fact Blackpool manager Simon Grayson.

As he did when appointing McAllister, Bates acted swiftly and decisively. On Monday he made his move for Grayson, but Blackpool rejected the approach. On Tuesday Grayson tendered his resignation, but Blackpool rejected that too. On Wednesday Leeds announced Grayson as their new manager regardless, and Blackpool announced they would be taking legal action against Bates, which was like water off a duck's back. On Thursday it was Christmas Day, and on Friday Grayson would fulfil his lifelong dream, in a fixture he couldn't have hand-picked better.

———

Leeds United 1 Leicester City 1

Matchday 22 of 46
Elland Road (33,580)

> *'The phone call came on Sunday dinnertime, "Would you want to be the next Leeds United manager?" I nearly choked on my roast beef! This was my dream job.'* – Simon Grayson

'Rocco is ... better than Simon Greyson' was my status on Facebook when McAllister's replacement was hurriedly announced. I was underwhelmed and had expected a higher-profile and more ambitious appointment, however, misspelling the new manager's name was a fitting representation of my ignorance and the more I read about Grayson the more I came around to the idea.

I knew Grayson had come through the youth team at Leeds but I hadn't realised he was Leeds through and through, and the fact he had resigned in protest at not being allowed to drop a division was a great way to announce himself at Elland Road. I was also enthused when reading about his impressive start in management. Having steered Blackpool clear of relegation trouble as player and caretaker manager, Grayson took the reins full-time in 2006/07 and his first full season ended with a sensational ten-match winning run to catapult the Tangerines into and then successfully through the play-offs, and into the Championship. At 39 years old Grayson was a hot young prospect in management, and after consolidating Blackpool in the Championship he was ready to take the next step forward in his career, which turned out to be a step back to League One, to his old club Leeds.

My initial scepticism had parted, but it was only when I first heard Grayson speak that I started to believe he was the right man to take Leeds up. He spoke with a clear understanding of, and passion for the job in hand. And the job in hand didn't stop at promotion to the Championship: 'Somebody is going to take this club back to the Premier League, and I want that man to be me.' In the short term, Grayson wasn't shying away from the responsibility on his shoulders. He could have legitimately pointed to the weaknesses that cost McAllister his job but instead he laid down the gauntlet to the squad he inherited, 'I know what League One is all about and I would like to think we have an opportunity to do what Blackpool did. The group of players here are more than capable of doing it.'

Grayson's first game was a Boxing Day clash against Leicester City, the club he had left Leeds to join as a 22-year-old, and where he had spent his best playing days, making over 200 appearances. This was a clash of the two biggest clubs in the division, and with Leicester clear at the top it was going to be a very difficult challenge for a team so low on confidence. After McAllister's struggles to nail down his best team I was intrigued to see what the new man would do, and the first name on the team sheet was a great start. Casper Ankergren's confidence had been undermined by sharing the goalkeeping duties with David Lucas but a new manager brings a clean slate and I was confident he'd recapture his best form. The back four was just as I would have picked it too: Richardson and Sheehan as full-backs, Rui Marques and Michalík centre-backs. It seemed a decent and balanced back four. The midfield looked well balanced with Grayson choosing the experience and know-how of Prutton, Douglas and Robinson alongside the teenage ace in his pack, Fabian Delph. The front two was a no-brainer – Beckford and Becchio – and with a bench containing Howson, Kilkenny, Hughes and Snodgrass, Leeds looked in much better shape than the league table suggested.

As well as a new manager to galvanise them, the players also had a bumper crowd on their side. With the east upper open, a crowd of approaching 35,000 was expected for the only Elland Road fixture of the festive period. Grayson was living the dream.

Simon Grayson: 'Walking out of the tunnel to "Marching on Together" was surreal, a moment I'll never forget. The Boxing Day fixture is a special day in the football calendar anyway, and to be testing ourselves against the best team in the division, my old team Leicester, made it even more magical.'

The Grayson era almost got off to the perfect start but Becchio was denied by the post, and shortly afterwards Leicester took the lead. There were no moans and groans though; the fans had wiped the slate clean too and the biggest Elland Road crowd of the season roared Grayson's team on. It helped that they liked what they saw.

As exciting as it had been to see McAllister's team in full flow, it was refreshing to see a more direct approach from Leeds. They played in a traditional 4-4-2 with a focus on feeding the wide players and getting crosses into the box, but they weren't afraid to get the ball forward quickly either, sending long 'passes' (as Grayson liked to call them) up to Becchio, or into the channels for Beckford to chase.

It was a very encouraging performance from a rejuvenated side, but as time ticked away an ignominious, albeit unfortunate, sixth straight defeat crept ever closer. Leeds kept fighting and finally got their reward in stoppage time, and the new manager was directly involved in conjuring up the equaliser. With 13 minutes remaining Grayson had introduced Howson and Snodgrass, and right at the death Howson clipped a beautiful ball to the far post which landed perfectly into the stride of Snodgrass, who converted from two yards to send the Kop, and his team-mates and manager, into raptures.

Jonny Howson: 'Moments like that lift everyone. Last-minute goals always mean that much more, and Grayson had a real knack of making changes that affected the game. Big moments can lead on to another, and suddenly you start to get that confidence back.'

It was only a single point on the board and Leeds remained ninth, but with the substitutes combining to rescue the game so late, Grayson must have felt on top of the world and probably deserved the man of the match champagne himself. 'You live

and die by those decisions,' said Grayson afterwards, and it
certainly felt like new life had been breathed into the season.
What a difference a day makes, and my Facebook status
reflected a shameless change of tack, 'Rocco is ... walking in
a Grayson wonderland.'

———

Leeds United 2 Southend United 0

Matchday 27 of 46
Elland Road (20,392)

> *'I wanted an out-and-out centre-back who would head it,
> tackle, and be a leader. Naylor ticked all those boxes, and
> being a supporter of Leeds United, he was perfect.' – Simon
> Grayson*

Simon Grayson's first victory came in his second match at
the helm, 3-1 away to Stockport County, with Fabian Delph
further enhancing his blossoming reputation by scoring the all-
important second goal with an exquisite 45-yard lob. Leading
into the January transfer window the teenager was attracting
lots of Premier League attention, though the two bids that
came in were not just rejected but ridiculed by Ken Bates, 'I
told both clubs that we do not deal in petty cash.'

With the transfer window open and no game for two
weeks (due to a frozen pitch at Hereford and a lack of FA Cup
duty) all eyes were on Leeds's transfer activity, with Grayson
roundly expected to prioritise signing a defender to stabilise
a shaky defence. However, the new manager was keen to give
the current players an opportunity to prove themselves, so
it stood to reason that first through the door was Bradley
Johnson, recalled from his loan at Brighton where he had been
in impressive form, scoring five goals in ten games.

Jonny Howson: 'You always knew what you were going to get with Brad. He'd give everything he's got every day, every game, and I love playing with players like that. And that's before you even get to the technical side.'

Grayson's first dip into the transfer market came after a blood clot was discovered on Enoch Showunmi's lung, consigning the striker to the sidelines for the foreseeable future – a cruel and scary blow. Showunmi's replacement was Lee Trundle, who had been a sensation at Swansea in the lower leagues but since stepping up to the Championship with Bristol City he had scored just eight goals in 57 games. Now 32, there were question marks about Trundle's physical condition, and with his career seemingly in decline this was a gamble by Grayson, but a short-term loan for a box-of-tricks striker who just might hit a purple patch seemed to be a worthwhile punt. I couldn't wait to see Trundle strutting his stuff at Elland Road.

Trundle made his debut from the bench the day after arriving in Yorkshire, but there was disappointment as Leeds were floored by a blast from the past. Michael Bridges returned to Elland Road for the first time in nine years and scored in a 2-0 win for Carlisle United, with former loanee Danny Graham scoring the other. Grayson had seen enough. 'Certain things were confirmed in my mind,' he said after the defeat, and his re-shaping of the squad accelerated over the course of the next week. Out went Mansour Assoumani, Paul Telfer, Ian Westlake and Malcolm Christie, all released from their contracts, while Peter Sweeney and Alan Sheehan were sent out on loan.

The outgoings opened the door for defensive reinforcements, which came in the form of Carl Dickinson and Richard Naylor. Dickinson was a 21-year-old left-back on loan from Stoke City who had been limited to two starts following promotion to the Premier League. He had also played under Grayson at

Blackpool, so this seemed a solid acquisition. As did Richard Naylor, an experienced, no-nonsense centre-back who arrived on loan from Ipswich Town, where he had spent his whole career, making over 300 appearances. Like his new manager, Naylor was Leeds through and through, and just before his 32nd birthday he finally had his dream move, 'My family are all in Ipswich now so it was a big decision, I think it took me ten seconds!' It would prove to be an inspired signing by Grayson. Naylor was a model professional who knew exactly what Leeds United was all about, and such was his impact he would be appointed captain even before he made his initial 30-day loan move permanent.

The new signings all started in the next match at Brighton, and the new defenders helped secure a first clean sheet since the first day of November, while Lee Trundle popped up with the crucial opening goal on the hour. In the closing stages Delph enhanced his reputation again by carrying the ball the length of the pitch before scoring with a 20-yard curler to seal a 2-0 win in style. 'As a team they are coming to understand what I want from them,' said a delighted Grayson. 'Defenders take no prisoners, and you can show your quality at the other end.' When he expands on his philosophy, it is clear to see the club had a Leeds United-minded person in charge.

> *Simon Grayson: 'We wanted to play nice football in the right areas but we wanted to be hard-working and disciplined, because that's a given when you play for Leeds United. You have to work hard for the badge, for the shirt, and for the supporters, but obviously entertain at the same time.'*

Grayson's first home victory came next, an impressive 3-1 win over Darren Ferguson's third-placed Peterborough United. All the goals came in an exhilarating final half an hour, with the returning Beckford opening the scoring within three minutes of his introduction from the bench before adding a clinical second shortly afterwards. Gary McAllister could have been forgiven for wondering just what might have been if Beckford hadn't pulled his hamstring a week before the calamitous trip to Histon.

Three days later Naylor fulfilled two lifelong dreams. Not only did he lead Leeds out at Elland Road, he also got himself on the scoresheet as Southend United were beaten 2-0. Naylor's goal came after only 11 minutes, by which time his centre-back partner, Rui Marques, had already opened the scoring, and after building the early lead the defenders then made sure it was protected securely. With Naylor winning every header the defence was transformed, and so too was the midfield. With Johnson and Snodgrass out wide, and Douglas and Delph in the centre, Grayson had found a perfect mix of flair and tenacity, and Leeds's confidence was restored.

> *Jermaine Beckford: 'I really loved Grayson's simplified approach. There were no square pegs in round holes, Simon played people where he would get eight out of ten from them, rather than trying to fit them into a certain system and getting seven out of ten.'*

The pre-Christmas fragility seemed to have been resolved almost overnight. Grayson was moulding a team that could outplay and outbattle their opponents, striking the balance between Dennis Wise's often turgid direct football and McAllister's determination to play his way out of the league. United were still five points adrift of the play-off places, but three wins on the bounce capped a great first month for Grayson.

Hereford United 2 Leeds United 0
Matchday 31 of 46
Edgar Street (6,120)

'Certain games can define how things work out, and Hereford was probably the perfect place to get beat. We didn't want to be coming back to that crumbling dressing room again.' –
Simon Grayson

Simon Grayson's second month was a great disappointment. The honeymoon period was over and Leeds's old problems resurfaced. February was a carbon copy of October, the month McAllister's rut set in, with three home wins and three away defeats. An early strike from Troy Deeney condemned Leeds to defeat at Walsall, but they bounced back with a 2-0 home win against Millwall, broadcast live on *Monday Night Football*. Thankfully the match went off without any violence off the pitch, but there was some on it when Jermaine Beckford – whose wonderful brace secured the points – swung an elbow into the face of the Millwall goalkeeper David Forde while waiting for a corner to be taken. The referee only issued a yellow card at the time, but with the Sky cameras providing damning evidence the FA reviewed the footage and gave Beckford a three-match suspension, this despite the rule book stating that any incident handled by the referee could not be revisited retrospectively (apparently, according to the referee's match report he had booked Beckford for pushing, not elbowing).

Without their suspended talisman, Leeds fell to another 1-0 defeat at Huddersfield. It was the day young goalkeeper Alex Smithies came of age, gaining vindication for his abysmal performance at Elland Road in the previous season by keeping the Whites at bay during a late onslaught. It was a horrible experience for me and Paul – we failed to get a ticket in the Leeds end and were instead sat with the most partisan Town fans, including our delirious friends Billy and Edwin. It was the first time Huddersfield had done the double over Leeds in 77 years.

Three days later Leeds headed to relegation-doomed Hereford United for what turned out to be a pivotal match. In front of 6,000 fans packed into Edgar Street, the lowest attendance of the Whites' League One adventure, they slipped to their ninth away defeat of the season (only four teams had lost more). It may have been different had Lee Trundle converted a first-half penalty, but two minutes after he missed Hereford took the lead and the visitors never recovered. 'WE'RE SHIT, AND WE'RE SICK OF IT!' rang out from the away end in the closing minutes, and after the final whistle the players were booed off the pitch and further lamented by the 2,000 travelling fans, who chanted, 'YOU'RE NOT FIT TO WEAR THE SHIRT!' Grayson probably didn't need to expand too much on the message from the terraces but just six weeks into his reign he decided to take the bull by the horns and, according to reports from the time, locked the players in the dressing room and read them the riot act. Grayson's account is a little less dramatic.

> *Simon Grayson: 'I felt it was my job to address it. We had a constructive and open chat. There were a few home truths but ultimately we told the players there were two ways this was going to go. Either we bury our heads in the sand and accept the supporters are right in what they are singing to us, or we stick our chests out, come out fighting, and show everybody that we're a united group who can still achieve what we set out to do.'*

Casper Ankergren's memories of the evening also suggest the dressing room lock-in was not as scathing as legend would have us believe. Either that, or it had been so traumatising that he'd successfully repressed the memories.

> *Casper Ankergren: 'I'll be honest with you, I don't remember that Hereford game at all!'*

Jermaine Beckford remembers very well, and his account suggests Casper had indeed repressed the memories.

> *Jermaine Beckford: 'Everyone knows what a lovely person Simon Grayson is, and up to that point that's all we'd seen. But at Hereford, wow man, he went for it! He was not holding back! But I really appreciated that. Although we knew what a nice guy he was, we also knew he could cut through us and bring us down to earth with a bump, within the blink of an eye. That's what you need as a player to keep you focussed.'*

The defeat proved to be the turning point of the season. Further to the dressing room lock-in, Grayson's more practical solution to Leeds's problems was to recall Jonathan Douglas, adding nous to a young midfield which contained 19-year-old Fabian Delph, 20-year-old Jonny Howson, 21-year-old Robert Snodgrass, 22-year-old Bradley Johnson and 23-year-old Neil Kilkenny. Four days later Leeds bounced back with a 2-0 victory over Cheltenham Town, Howson grabbing both goals. Another home win followed, the fifth in a row at Elland Road, but the most pleasing aspect was the fortitude shown by the team, who prevailed against Scunthorpe despite the disappointment of surrendering a 2-0 lead, and leapfrogged Nigel Adkins's men, moving into the play-off places for the first time under Grayson.

—

Oldham Athletic 1 Leeds United 1

Matchday 34 of 46
Boundary Park (7,835)

> *'If you're wearing a Leeds United shirt everyone expects you to be mature, physically strong, with the right mentality.*

Age doesn't seem to be taken into account.' – Jermaine Beckford

Fixtures were coming thick and fast, and three days after the victory over Scunthorpe, Leeds had the chance to leapfrog another promotion rival when they visited fourth-placed Oldham. The fans were feeling positive again, but a fourth successive away defeat would be a hammer blow to Grayson's progress. Thus, it was a real relief to leave Oldham with a point on the board, especially after Leeds fell behind in the second half to a goal from former West Bromwich Albion goal machine, and convicted killer, Lee Hughes, whose hit and run crime cost a man his life and Hughes three years of his career. Had he reported the accident his victim may have lived, but by fleeing the scene the prosecution were unable to prove he was drunk behind the wheel, and not just driving 'like a madman'. It was sickening to see him celebrating on the pitch.

Grayson's team again displayed their new-found mettle by responding immediately, although it was barely a team effort; the equaliser was all down to Delph. Like a stroppy teenager, annoyed at his team-mates for conceding a goal, Delph took it upon himself to surge forward with the ball straight from the kick-off. He dribbled all the way through to the Oldham box, not quite scoring but winning a corner, from which Becchio scored to the delight of the travelling fans behind the goal.

If there was an element of teenage stroppiness about Delph's dribble, perhaps it was born out of the frustration of losing his place in the heart of midfield, despite playing so well. Grayson had shunted the jewel in his crown out to the left wing to incorporate Jonathan Douglas, a decision that stifled Delph's influence on matches but succeeded in eradicating the soft underbelly that had plagued the season. As Delph's form dipped, the team's form soared.

Simon Grayson: 'I wanted more control in midfield while keeping Jermaine and Luciano up front. Delph was a hugely talented central midfielder, who would clearly go on to have a fantastic career, but I knew he would still contribute from the left with his ability on the ball, and with goals and assists. I wanted my main players in the final third where they would have the freedom to express themselves and make things happen.'

Faced with another tricky away game at Bristol Rovers, goals from Becchio and Snodgrass seemed to have secured a long-awaited away win, but a gut-wrenching injury-time equaliser ensured another miserable journey home for the travelling fans and knocked Leeds out of the play-off places again. But not for long. A return to the home comforts of Elland Road brought two wins in four days, a 4-0 midweek thrashing of Yeovil and a resilient 1-0 win against Swindon. These two games were chalk and cheese performances but they each brought three points, and acted as a prime example of Grayson's willingness to change the approach of his side.

Bradley Johnson: 'There was going to be games where you can't play teams off the park and you need to be aggressive. Grayson adapted to each team, he knew the league and was willing to mix it up.'

Leeds finally gave their travelling army something to cheer about by overcoming Crewe Alexandra 3-2. It was Grayson's first away victory in over two months, yet the manager was seething after his side almost surrendered a 3-0 lead. 'It feels like we have drawn or lost the game, that's how frustrated I am with the performance,' fumed Grayson. 'We have set ourselves high standards and I want us to reach those standards all the time.' The sloppy end to the match proved to be a blessing in disguise, as it led to the arrival of another central defender, Sam Sodje, on an emergency loan (a Ken Bates trademark). Sodje quickly formed a rock-solid partnership with Richard Naylor which proved to be the final piece in Grayson's jigsaw, with neither Rui Marques nor Ľubomír Michalík proving to be reliable enough week in, week out. Each had been a fan favourite at one time, but that seemed a long time ago now.

Sodje completed an all-new back four following injuries to full-backs Frazer Richardson and Carl Dickinson. Grayson had resolved those problems internally by giving another Thorp Arch prospect, Ben Parker, his chance to stake a claim for the left-back slot, with Jonathan Douglas the surprise solution at right-back. Beckford saw the value of having players like Douglas in the team, whatever position they filled.

> *Jermaine Beckford: 'We had a lot of inexperience and maybe some immaturity as well, and that's why it was so beneficial to have the experienced players like David Prutton, Richard Naylor, and especially Johnny Douglas, who was one of the nicest people I've ever met – on his good days! But he also had that spike. Being a little older than the rest of us made a huge difference, you had to look up to him, you had to listen to him, and you didn't want to be on the end of one of his rants! We learnt more from listening to the experienced players than we ever could from learning on the job.'*

Compared to the erratic form of the team this season, it had been quite a serene season off the pitch, with little in terms of Ken Bates sagas. A charge for illegal payments to agents here, a complaint for poaching managers there, and an ongoing battle to get the council to pay for, or at least permit, his exuberant East Stand redevelopment plans – it wasn't really enough to stave off boredom for our chairman, stuck in his tax haven in Monaco. A magnet for conflict, if Bates wasn't attracting any he seemed to seek it out, and he duly found an opportunity to engage in more legal wrangling when Sheffield United were awarded £20m in compensation from West Ham United after their illegal signing, Carlos Tevez, relegated Neil Warnock's men in 2007. What's that got to do with Leeds, you ask? Well, Bates wanted a chunk of the money as he'd missed out on bonus payments for the sales of Rob Hulse and Matthew Kilgallon, which would have been triggered had the Blades survived in the Premier League.

It was a shot from the hip that amounted to nothing, but Bates was now back in the groove and settled two more long-running sagas in early April. First to close was the dispute with Blackpool over Grayson's appointment, with Leeds reportedly paying £200,000 in compensation, and then came the 'exciting' news that Leeds City Council had finally granted planning permission for the East Stand redevelopment. 'The development is designed to increase non-matchday income streams at Elland Road,' explained Bates. 'It won't take anything away from the club's ambitious plans on the pitch.' To the fans these reassuring words were just hot air – they would always be sceptical of anything that came out of their chairman's mouth.

———

Leicester City 1 Leeds United 0

Matchday 43 of 46
Walkers Stadium (27,507)

> *'Grayson brought different ideas. He helped change the dynamic and get better results, which obviously began to give confidence to the team and to me too.' – Luciano Becchio*

Victories over MK Dons and Colchester United made it five wins on the bounce, and four clean sheets within that run was almost as pleasing. By hook or by crook Grayson had assembled a fully functioning defence, and now I wasn't just dreaming of promotion, I was expecting it. The MK Dons game had extra significance for Beckford, who scored his 50th goal for the club, in under 100 appearances.

> *Jermaine Beckford: 'Reaching 50 goals in all competitions for Leeds United was a milestone I never in a million years thought I would achieve. So when I got it, although I didn't mention it to anyone, inside I was absolutely buzzing.'*

The successive wins generated speculation about whether Grayson could repeat the ten-match winning streak that took his Blackpool team to promotion. If Leeds could win all their remaining games they would likely snatch automatic promotion, but the dream died abruptly in the next match at Brisbane Road, when ten-man Leyton Orient battled back from two goals down to salvage a draw with a late equaliser.

Leeds bounced back from that disappointment with a 1-0 win over Stockport County, and with four games remaining they had little chance of avoiding the play-offs. The 75 points already amassed would usually be enough for a top-six finish, and they trailed second-placed Peterborough United by seven points. Only by winning every match would Leeds stand even a slim chance of overhauling Darren Ferguson's team, and next up was a trip to Leicester, the champions elect, who could seal promotion with a victory.

They may have been the best team in the league, but the Foxes didn't concern me as much as the city of Leicester, where Leeds fans had rarely had the last laugh in my lifetime. Between my first trip to Filbert Street in 1997, and my last in 2002, Leeds missed a last-minute penalty to equalise, conceded two injury-time goals to be knocked out of the League Cup, lost on penalties in that same competition, lost a game that ended their Premier League title challenge, conceded three goals in the first 30 minutes of Rio Ferdinand's debut, and even when I finally saw us win there, the abuse I received from the home fans tarnished a 6-0 victory! Filbert Street was no more, but things barely improved at the Walkers Stadium. Leeds's first visit ended in a 4-0 thrashing on the way to relegation from the Premier League, and on the way to relegation from the Championship we conceded an equaliser while still celebrating and goading the home fans after Robbie Blake had put Leeds ahead. Leicester fans always had the last laugh.

In all likelihood this game would end up being a dead rubber, but there was more than pride at stake for the Leeds players. In the fabled Hereford dressing room, Simon Grayson had challenged his team to go undefeated through the last 15 games of the season, and if they could get through this match unscathed they would likely achieve that quite remarkable feat. It was also an opportunity for United to show how far they had come under Grayson, and that was clear to see on a lovely sunny day in the East Midlands. The Whites put up a good fight in a good match between two good teams, the best two teams in the division. Sodje and Naylor looked impenetrable at the back, and Douglas and Parker handled two very tricky wingers – Lloyd Dyer and Max Gradel – impressively. Kilkenny and Howson controlled the midfield, but in the absence of the injured Jermaine Beckford, up front it just wasn't clicking, with new loan signing Liam Dickinson looking painfully out of his depth. Consequently, Leeds struggled to fully assert themselves.

And so to the inevitable last laugh. With a solid 0-0 draw about to be achieved, Gradel crossed from the right and substitute Steve Howard rose highest at the back post to head in an injury-time winner. Bloody Leicester. The ground erupted, and their promotion was all but secured, though not mathematically until the afternoon's matches had taken place.

This fixture had been moved forward to a lunchtime kick-off on police advice and their cautious approach seemed well-placed shortly after the full-time whistle, when the Leicester fans added their name to a small list of clubs who have goaded Leeds over the tragic killing of their supporters in Istanbul. The heinous chants still drew an incensed response from Leeds supporters, nearly a decade on, but the Leicester faithful didn't seem to realise the seriousness of their crime. They looked stunned as the away end erupted in fury, with dozens of Leeds fans charging towards them and clambering over the segregational netting. The police were on hand to prevent a serious incident, but the bitter taste of an injury-time defeat had been compounded.

As we headed back up the M1 we listened to talkSPORT, which further compounded our misery. Peterborough fell to defeat, meaning Leeds had missed a glorious chance to make a late dash for automatic promotion. Furthermore, with Scunthorpe and Tranmere both winning, the door was now ajar for the chasing pack in the rear-view mirror. Tranmere in sixth trailed Leeds by three points, and Scunthorpe in seventh trailed by five points but had two games in hand. Grayson's team still had work to do.

Leeds United 3 Northampton Town 0
Matchday 46 of 46
Elland Road (34,214)

> *'Under Grayson we were a lot more organised. Sodje was great alongside Naylor, he won everything in the air.'* – Casper Ankergren

Leeds bounced back in impressive fashion by all but cementing their place in the play-offs with a 3-1 win over their closest challengers, Tranmere Rovers. A 1-0 win at Hartlepool sealed the deal mathematically, so by the time Northampton arrived at Elland Road the only thing at stake was pride, and the chance to relegate another club that had voted for the 15-point deduction – a carbon copy of the last match of the previous season.

I wouldn't be there for the regular season's finale as instead I jetted off to Vegas. We'd managed to get tickets for Ricky Hatton's world title fight against Manny Pacquiao although the weigh-in was the highlight of the trip. The fight itself was a disaster. A 30-hour, 10,000-mile round trip, to watch less than two rounds of boxing. I'll never forget the shrieks and whoops of the Filipino supporters when Hatton was knocked spark out.

Back at Elland Road, in front of the biggest crowd of the season, the Whites signed off the regular season with a comfortable 3-0 victory over relegated Northampton and set up a play-off semi-final with Millwall, an outcome the authorities must have been dreading. That said, two semi-finals may have been preferable to 90,000 rival supporters descending on Wembley. Significantly, Millwall's final-day defeat allowed Leeds to leapfrog the Lions, meaning Grayson's men would have home advantage in the all-important second leg. This was a mouthwatering prospect for me, as the previous play-off home games had been first legs, as had the Champions League semi-final, which seemed a lifetime ago now.

Leeds were heading into the play-offs as the division's form side, and with a fully fit Jermaine Beckford scoring in each of the last three fixtures they were looking unstoppable. Beckford had reached new heights this season, almost scoring at a rate of a goal a game to reach a staggering 34 goals despite his injury problems. Plenty of credit for his goalscoring exploits could be given to the brutality of Becchio, a battering ram that opposition defenders couldn't contain, who himself was edging towards 20 goals for the season, but Beckford was the star man. He was firmly established as one of the leading marksmen outside the Premier League, and also as a leader in the dressing room.

> *Bradley Johnson: 'I've never played with a striker as ruthless as Becks. The goals speak for themselves but Jermaine scored all sorts of goals; outside the box, inside the box, left foot, right foot, headers. He was deadly. He was a leader in the changing room too, he was huge for us, and one of the most down to earth people you'd ever meet. Becks would come in every day and say hello to everyone and shake their hand, the canteen staff, everyone.'*

Leeds may have been the clear favourites to win the play-offs, but within the club you would never hear such confidence. Leeds United and the play-offs do not mix, and the mental anguish of three previous defeats in finals resulted in many supporters writing off their chances. Despite my own eternal pessimism, I could see no way of losing to Millwall. Similar to the second half of the previous season, the new manager had successfully implemented his style on the players, but Grayson's team were a different kettle of fish to McAllister's. They had a rock-solid defence and a 50-goal strike force, plus, the law of averages was on their side. Surely this time Leeds would prevail.

—

Millwall 1 Leeds United 0

Play-off semi-final first leg
The Den (13,228)

> *'We went into the play-offs full of confidence, but we weren't getting ahead of ourselves. We knew Millwall was a difficult place to go.' – Simon Grayson*

Rather than splurging money on a trip to London with the potential of another London trip only weeks away, I didn't bother applying for the first leg of the play-offs at The Den – renamed with 'New' removed. The lunchtime kick-off made Millwall away even less attractive than normal, and a reduced allocation for away fans in each leg – to a maximum of 1,000 to limit the potential for trouble – made my decision even easier, and probably took it out of my hands regardless.

Instead, I headed to The Alex, which I hoped would prove a lucky charm after watching the previous season's epic semi-final in the same venue. In fact, all play-off semi-finals that Leeds United had been involved in had resulted in epic wins. In the first promotion play-offs in 1987, Leeds conceded in the 89th minute at Oldham before scoring in the 90th minute to reach the final on away goals. In 2006, Leeds won a crazy second leg at Preston with only nine men, and then there was 2008's last-gasp win at Carlisle. OK, Leeds had lost all the finals, but for a club with a sworn hatred for the play-offs these were some pretty special memories.

Try telling Millwall about Leeds's bad record in the play-offs and they would laugh in your face. The south Londoners had failed to win any of their eight play-off matches, though their manager Kenny Jackett, like Leeds, had reached the final in all three play-off campaigns he had been involved in. Jackett sprung a surprise with his team selection, leaving the club's record goalscorer Neil Harris on the bench, but there were no surprises from Grayson, who made no changes and kept faith with a young midfield that had an average age of just 20: Snodgrass, Howson, Kilkenny and Delph. It was a tough time for David Prutton, who had found himself out in the cold and not even on the bench for the defining matches of the season.

David Prutton: 'Simon liked consistency and a low-maintenance dressing room. He would pick the same team most weeks and if the team does well he doesn't have to answer any questions. If you're not in that 11 and the team's doing well, there's absolutely nothing you can say!'

It was a tense battle on the pitch and a hostile atmosphere in the stands, resulting in a bad-tempered and very niggly first half. There were flare-ups, hard tackles flying in at every opportunity and more injuries than chances as the game struggled to find a rhythm, and at half-time the teams trudged off goalless.

A 0-0 draw would have done quite nicely for Leeds and the home side were clearly fully aware of this as they cranked up their performance in the second half; so too did the home fans. Roared on by a partisan crowd, Millwall were firmly on the front foot and substitute Harris came close to opening the scoring with a clever flick that Ankergren was equal to. Harris didn't have to wait much longer to put Millwall in the lead. With 70 minutes on the clock a hopeful cross into the box was completely misjudged by Richard Naylor, and with ample time and space to adjust his feet, Harris fired past Ankergren to spark wild scenes of celebration at The Den, as over-excited fans spilled on to the pitch.

Perhaps the Leeds players were a little rattled. They failed to muster any type of response and the Lions saw out a 1-0 victory to claim the advantage heading into the second leg at Elland Road. Grayson's team hadn't played badly, but the fact Sam Sodje was their man of the match told a story. Sodje had put in a colossal performance, but the highlight of his afternoon came when he dislocated his shoulder only to pop it back into place with the help of the physio, and play out the final 15 minutes like nothing had happened. What a warrior. The Met police showed a similar disregard for a potentially serious incident when praising the conduct of the Millwall supporters, despite the pitch invasion following

Harris's goal, during which Ankergren had allegedly been assaulted.

> *Casper Ankergren: 'I wouldn't call it assaulted! They ran on the pitch, which they shouldn't have done, a few words were said but that was it.'*

The FA launched an investigation into the incident but Simon Grayson was quick to play it down: 'In play-off semi-finals the atmosphere is quite hostile and people get exuberant. My players are OK and nothing much was made of it. I wouldn't want to take Casper on if I was a Millwall fan anyway!'

I was of course disappointed by the result, but not disheartened. Millwall had given everything just to claim a scrappy win by the slenderest of margins, and they would surely be no match for Leeds in the return leg in five days' time, under the lights in front of a sell-out crowd at fortress Elland Road.

> *Simon Grayson: 'Losing the first game 1-0, while it wasn't ideal, it wasn't the end of the world. Going back to a full Elland Road, backed by an electric atmosphere, we felt like we had a great opportunity.'*

Leeds United 1 Millwall 1
Play-off semi-final second leg
Elland Road (37,036)

> *'That noise. It was awesome. It was deafening. I'll never forget it.'* – Luciano Becchio

Heading into the return leg the mood in the Leeds camp was optimistic. United had won their previous 11 games at Elland

Road and boasted the best home record in the entire Football League, but it was unnerving to know that anything less than a win would mean a third season in the third tier. And even a win might not be enough. Leeds needed to win by two clear goals to reach Wembley – a one-goal victory would result in a penalty shoot-out, and nobody wanted that.

As they had in the previous season's play-off home leg, Leeds lost the toss and were made to attack the Kop in the first half. Knowing they only had these 45 minutes to suck the ball into the net, the Kop was perhaps even more vociferous than it might have otherwise been. Thunderous tackles flew in almost from kick-off resulting in another fragmented half of football, although the home side were in the ascendancy throughout, playing at a high tempo that revealed their desperation to get back on level terms. However, Millwall defended resolutely, restricting Leeds to only one chance of note, when Beckford's drive was parried by the keeper and Delph's rebound landed safely in his arms. At the other end it was a case of waiting all half for a shot and then two coming at once, though both were long-range efforts that ballooned into the South Stand. Nevertheless, at half-time Millwall were halfway there.

Straight from kick-off the onslaught began, and before Millwall could obtain any possession referee Mark Halsey had awarded Leeds a penalty. It was the third time Sam Sodje had been bundled to the floor as a cross was sent into the box, and the fans were so shocked to see the offence punished that it took an eternity for Elland Road to rejoice. Beckford was already guaranteed to finish the season as English football's top goalscorer and stepped up with the chance of notching goal number 35, but his weak spot kick was saved.

Jermaine Beckford: 'I thought everyone had forgot about that! Cheers man, I'd put those demons to bed!'

The reason people might have forgotten about the penalty miss was because redemption came just three minutes later, thanks to Ben Parker. In his breakthrough season, the 21-year-old had made the left-back spot his own and produced the highlight of his career. Parker ended a rare Millwall foray into the Leeds half by tracking back and intercepting a through ball inside his own box, then, under pressure from the attacker, he calmly turned his man and set off up the left wing. Roared on by an Elland Road crowd that was becoming more and more desperate, Parker passed to Beckford out on the touchline, who cleverly flicked the ball on to Andy Robinson while Parker continued his run, and as the crowd's roar intensified so too did Parker's speed. Robinson played the ball perfectly into his path, and after a 70-yard dash, Parker drilled a brilliant low ball into the corridor of uncertainty, where Luciano Becchio had ghosted between the centre-backs to slide home his 19th and most important goal of the season. The loudest I had ever heard Elland Road was when Lee Bowyer's 89th-minute drive squirmed into the AC Milan net in the Champions League, but that was demoted to second place amid the wild and bloodthirsty wall of noise that greeted Becchio's equaliser, in the 51st minute of a third-tier match.

Leeds were firmly in the ascendancy; the crowd was super-charged and victory seemed a formality. However, a 'missile' thrown at the Millwall goalkeeper by an exuberant fan, and a suspiciously convenient three-minute break for a head injury that was subsequently 'run off', gave the visitors some breathing space. Simon Grayson felt the significance of that moment.

Simon Grayson: 'We had played really well and Becchio's goal lifted the roof off. Elland Road was rocking and Millwall couldn't live with us, but whether it was gamesmanship or not, the head injury blew the wind out of our sails and we lost momentum. I'm sure we'd have got the second goal but for that stoppage in play.'

Like a boxer saved by the bell, the visitors had survived and began to find their feet, and in the 73rd minute they delivered a sucker punch. A deep cross into the Leeds box was knocked back across goal by substitute Lewis Grabban and knocked into the net by the unmarked Jimmy Abdou. It was one of fewer than a dozen goals the midfielder would score in 400 games in England, and it was Millwall's only shot on target, coming from their only venture into Leeds's penalty box. It proved to be a knockout blow. Elland Road was shocked to the core, and their team never recovered.

Grayson threw Sam Sodje up front and Leeds huffed and puffed, but a robust Millwall back line was giving nothing away. The best Leeds could muster was a few corners from a series of long balls, until the 89th minute when Bradley Johnson unleashed a piledriver that flew towards the bottom corner but whistled inches past the post. When the net didn't bulge I knew that was it. There was still enough time, almost eight minutes of injury time were played, but the Millwall goal was never threatened and the final whistle signalled the end of Leeds's season.

'WE'RE LEEDS, AND WE'RE PROUD OF IT!' bellowed around the ground as the crestfallen players lay flat on their backs, while the euphoric Millwall squad celebrated with their small pocket of fans in the upper section of the 'cheese wedge' away end. They were on their way to Wembley, where none of them had ever seen their team play, unless they were as old as Ken Bates, who was 13 years old when Millwall lost 2-0 to Chelsea in the final of the 1945 Football League War Cup South.

Jonny Howson: 'This was Leeds and Millwall, who aren't the best of friends, and some of their players were walking round after, clapping the Leeds fans. I think it was a case of them realising what a special atmosphere they've just played in, because some of those lads won't have played in that before, and maybe wouldn't again.'

Once again, I was left with that familiar feeling of devastation as the team embarked upon a lap of honour, and the sight of Fabian Delph worshipping the Kop compounded my anguish. The realisation struck that this would probably be the last time he played at Elland Road in a Leeds shirt, and the sorry plight of my club really sunk in. We weren't going to Wembley, we weren't going up, and things were likely to get even worse before they got better. The Whites had given everything but had fallen short again. Another play-off defeat to add to the list, and another season as League One Leeds.

League One table 2008/09

	P	W	D	L	F	A	Pts
Leicester City	46	27	15	4	84	39	96
Peterborough United	46	26	11	9	78	54	89
Milton Keynes Dons	46	26	9	11	83	47	87
LEEDS UNITED	**46**	**26**	**6**	**14**	**77**	**49**	**84**
Millwall	46	25	7	14	63	53	82
Scunthorpe United (P)	46	22	10	14	82	63	76
Tranmere Rovers	46	21	11	14	62	49	74
Southend United	46	21	8	17	58	61	71
Huddersfield Town	46	18	14	14	62	65	68
Oldham Athletic	46	16	17	13	66	65	65
Bristol Rovers	46	17	12	17	79	61	63
Colchester United	46	18	9	19	58	58	63
Walsall	46	17	10	19	61	66	61
Leyton Orient	46	15	11	20	45	57	56
Swindon Town	46	12	17	17	68	71	53
Brighton & Hove Albion	46	13	13	20	55	70	52
Yeovil Town	46	12	15	19	41	66	51
Stockport County*	46	16	12	18	59	57	50
Hartlepool United	46	13	11	22	66	79	50
Carlisle United	46	12	14	20	56	69	50
Northampton Town	46	12	13	21	61	65	49
Crewe Alexandra	46	12	10	24	59	82	46
Cheltenham Town	46	9	12	25	51	91	39
Hereford United	46	9	7	30	42	79	34

*Stockport deducted 10 points

PART THREE: 2009/10

TO HELL AND BACK

INTRODUCTION

by Jermaine Beckford

Summer 2009 was an annoying time. I wanted to sign a new contract extension so myself and my agent had conversations with the club about extending my deal. I wasn't trying to be the highest-paid player at the club, but I did want to be appreciated for the work that I had done, for the influence I had on the team and for what I was going to do in the future. I was so excited and so happy at Leeds, and I wanted that to continue, especially after everything we'd been through.

I'd been to the play-off final in the Millennium Stadium and lost 3-0 to Watford, I'd been to Wembley and lost 1-0 to Doncaster, and I'd been to the play-off semi-finals and lost to Millwall. There was a lot to rectify and I wanted to right those wrongs. Unfortunately, the contract I was offered was unacceptable, with no negotiations allowed, so I went on the transfer list. As soon as we'd done it I hated the idea, I wanted to be taken off the transfer list that very same day. I didn't need the outside distractions of my agent telling me that this club or that club were interested in me, I didn't want to discuss it, I wasn't interested, because I didn't want to leave!

It was an uncomfortable position for me at the best of times, so I was taken off the list and left to knuckle down, and focus on what was going on within the white lines of the football pitch.

Burnley 1 Leeds United 2

Pre-season friendly
Turf Moor (7,899)

> *'We'd done really well since Christmas and needed to take the momentum into the new season. We wanted to be the ones celebrating, not licking our wounds again.'* – Simon Grayson

Having successfully re-structured the playing staff and ended the season so strongly, Leeds headed into their third League One campaign without the need for a major summer upheaval. It felt like a head start, just as beginning on zero points had done in the previous summer. However, this notion didn't account for the potential outgoings, and there was great concern surrounding the futures of the two stars of the team.

No Leeds player since the great John Charles had scored more goals in a season than Jermaine Beckford's latest tally of 34, but with only a year remaining on his contract and no agreement in sight he was placed on the transfer list two weeks after the play-off defeat. For the fans it was a bone of contention that Ken Bates had allowed his star striker to enter the final year of his contract in the first place, but he was soon removed from the transfer list, with all parties agreeing that Beckford would remain at Leeds for the final year of his contract with his future 'to be re-assessed at the end of the season'. We all knew what that meant, our goal machine would almost certainly walk away for nothing, but that would be much easier to swallow if he fired us back to the Championship first.

Meanwhile, the Premier League vultures were circling around Fabian Delph with great intent. In his debut season the teenager had made 51 appearances and cleaned up at the club's end-of-season awards, scooping the Young Player of the Year, Players' Player of the Year, and the Goal of the Season prizes. Delph was also named in the League One Team of the Year, and won the Football League's Young Player of the Season award. Such was his talent an exit felt inevitable, and in the final days of pre-season Aston Villa pipped Manchester City to the teenager's signature for £6m. What a sad day that was. For me, losing our best young talent was the hardest part of life as a lower-league club.

Delph wasn't the only significant exit from Elland Road. Frazer Richardson and Jonathan Douglas were the last remaining players on first-team Championship wages, but with both contracts now expired and Leeds still in League One the club were unable to agree new terms and wished them a fond farewell. Although it was frustrating to lose two former captains entering the prime of their careers – each with over 150 Leeds appearances – for nothing, the fans understood the predicament. However, the situation became difficult to comprehend when both players joined League One rivals.

It was a similar story with Sam Sodje, whose eight appearances for Leeds had been so impressive that he'd forced his way back into the Nigeria squad. Sodje was a free agent, but still Leeds couldn't afford him. Instead he joined Richardson at Charlton, which resulted in more accusing fingers pointing at Bates. Leeds had by far the largest turnover in the division, so why were we being outbid by our promotion rivals? Sodje was at least joining a club that was in his blood, not leaving one, like Richardson.

The outgoings were disappointing and the incomings were underwhelming. Goalkeeper Shane Higgs, 32, was brought in on a free transfer from relegated Cheltenham Town; right-back Jason Crowe, 30, came in on a free from relegated Northampton Town; and centre-back Patrick Kisnorbo, 28, was also a free, from promoted Leicester City. Few people could argue that the quality in Leeds's squad hadn't been downgraded, but my faith in Simon Grayson was unwavering, and if he was happy,

I was happy. And he was happy. He had a solid foundation of experienced pros, a young and talented midfield, and he still had his star striker.

> *Simon Grayson: 'Selling Delph meant we didn't need to sell Beckford, and Douglas and Richardson were on high wages so we used that money to strengthen in other areas ahead of a real slog of a season. I did try and sign Sodje because he was a great lad and a real good defender, but I'd always wanted Kisnorbo since playing against him at Leicester. In an ideal world, knowing Kisnorbo could play as a holding midfielder, I'd have signed them both.'*

There seemed no reason to be downbeat as Leeds ramped up to the season with three impressive results. Only a 90th-minute penalty denied them victory over Premier League Blackburn Rovers at Elland Road, then they battled to a 0-0 draw at Newcastle, before beating top-flight new boys Burnley 2-1 at Turf Moor. Regardless of the lack of cash spent, and the excess money recouped, it was clear that Grayson was beginning the season with a squad that had the potential to blow the division away.

Leeds United 2 Exeter City 1

Matchday 1 of 46
Elland Road (27,681)

> *'If you go through our team player for player – Howson more mature, Snodgrass, Beckford, Becchio, Kisnorbo – we had too good a team to be in that league, and I think we knew that.' – Casper Ankergren*

Grayson's line-up for the opening match of the season portrayed not only the strength of Leeds's team, but also their strength in depth. For starters, with Shane Higgs getting the nod in goal, Casper Ankergren could consider himself to be the greatest number two in League One history. Captain Richard Naylor's ever-present streak ended due to a back injury, so Angola international Rui Marques stepped in alongside Australia regular Kisnorbo, with Slovakian international Ľubomír Michalík promoted to the bench. Kisnorbo's compatriot, playmaker Neil Kilkenny, was unavailable, but there was still no place in midfield for two players in the prime of their careers who had already proved themselves at a higher level, Andy Hughes and David Prutton. Both had to settle for the bench, with Grayson preferring youngsters Howson, Snodgrass and Bradley Johnson, anchored by seasoned campaigner Michael Doyle, who had joined on a season-long loan from Coventry on the eve of the campaign.

> *Simon Grayson: 'I'd always wanted a dominant midfielder, like when I was a young player watching David Batty allowing Strachan, McAllister and Speed the freedom to go and win matches. Doyle was the glue that held the midfield together. He was the type of player that can be underestimated by supporters, who you only realise you miss when they aren't in the team.'*

The only area where Leeds didn't have competition for places was up front, but only because Beckford and Becchio were so good. Having like-for-like replacements for the best strikers in the division was unrealistic, but with Trésor Kandol back after successful loans at Millwall and Charlton, and American youngster Mike Grella now integrated into the squad, Grayson had a duo who offered competent cover at least.

It was a carnival atmosphere on a hot summer's day at Elland Road, with the Leeds fans expecting a result that would send a message to the rest of the division. Expectation levels rose as Beckford was presented with three chances inside the first 12 minutes. The first two were spurned, but when Ben Parker surged upfield in now trademark fashion, past three challenges before splitting the defence, Beckford would not be denied a third time. He finished with the composure and expertise of a top-class striker, waiting for the keeper to commit himself before dinking the ball over him and inside the far post.

> *Jermaine Beckford: 'I had the ability to slow everything down in the last two seconds before having a shot, play everything out in slow motion. I'd see the keeper committing himself, if he's going down I could lift it into the space vacated, or if he stands big there's a space between his legs. If there's no time at all you just leather it, but I wasn't very good at that!'*

'SIGN YOUR CONTRACT FOR THE LADS!' chanted the Kop, though I didn't join in. I hoped everyone would soon put the situation to the back of their minds and just let him crack on with getting us promoted.

At half-time it was still 1-0, but when Exeter were reduced to ten men for an elbow on Doyle the only question was how many Leeds would win by. The Exeter fans had travelled in great numbers, filling the 'cheese wedge' and half of the South Stand, and 15 minutes after the red card they were stunned into delirious celebration when a wonderful free kick found the top corner. The rest of Elland Road was stunned into silence.

Immediately Grayson introduced Andy Robinson from the bench. The Scouse winger had underwhelmed since arriving as one of the best-paid players in the squad, but he was the man entrusted to unlock a stubborn defence. It was finally unlocked in the 88th minute but the goal originated from the opposite flank, with Jason Crowe providing the overlap and a perfect cross on to the head of Beckford, who nodded into the net to bring about the first Elland Road Shuffle of the season. It was a scrappy victory but Leeds were up and running with three points on the board, which was all anybody cared about.

There was another scrappy victory in the following game, with Leeds winning their first ever match against Wycombe Wanderers thanks to a thunderbolt from Becchio, and the midweek trip to Walsall made it three scrappy wins out of three. The Whites had looked set for their first defeat of the season when Marques conceded a needless 80th-minute penalty, but Grayson's men stormed back with the response of champions. Within minutes Johnson had powered home a back-post header, and Beckford won the game with a stunning 25-yard shot, struck on the turn, out of nothing with his weaker left foot, leaving the keeper with no chance. The 4,000 travelling fans (making up almost half of the attendance) went wild, many of them celebrating on the pitch with the players. By hook or by crook, it had been a perfect start for Leeds.

—

Leeds United 2 Stockport County 0

Matchday 6 of 46
Elland Road (22,870)

> *'Our home record was unbelievable. With the fans behind us at Elland Road a lot of teams were intimidated and it worked in our favour.' – Bradley Johnson*

The third Saturday of the season brought John Barnes's Tranmere Rovers to Elland Road. I was in attendance for Barnes's first game in management, in July 1999 at Parkhead, when O'Leary's Babies trounced his Celtic team. The 2-1 scoreline did no justice to the dominance of Leeds's performance on that day, and the same could be said of the 3-0 result on this day. I could not remember such a one-sided match; at times it was comical as Tranmere's persistence in trying to play out from the back landed them in trouble time and again. 'We started exactly how we wanted, with a high tempo and really pressing them,' remarked Grayson after the match. 'I think Jermaine could have had a hat-trick within the first ten minutes, everything came together today.' The man known as 'Larry' was happy as Larry, while his opposite number bemoaned his struggling team. Six weeks later Barnes's managerial career would be over.

Barnes wasn't the first manager to lose his job this season. The managerial merry-go-round had started to turn on the opening day when Norwich sacked Bryan Gunn after a 7-1 defeat at home to Colchester United. Norwich had the last laugh though, dishing out the ultimate revenge by replacing Gunn with the man who masterminded their humiliation, Paul Lambert, so Colchester were managerless as they prepared to host Leeds.

Colchester's Layer Road stadium held awful memories for the Whites, most notably when Don Revie's great team lost there in the 1971 FA Cup while Colchester were in the Fourth Division. Leeds's other trip to Layer Road came on Easter Monday 2007, which was arguably even more painful. Dennis Wise's team looked set for a third straight victory, which would have taken them clear of the relegation zone, but a late equaliser and an injury-time winner was a killer blow they never recovered from. Thankfully Layer Road was no more, and the Colchester Community Stadium was very different surroundings, about as unintimidating as it sounds. Former Thorp Arch graduate Alan Maybury was feeling especially hospitable and handed the visitors all three points on a plate by setting up Beckford for a five-yard tap-in. Maybury never played for Colchester again.

Leeds headed into September with the opportunity to set two new club records. Their five wins in the league, together with victories over Darlington and Watford in the League Cup, had equalled the club's best start to a season – seven wins in a row – a record Grayson now shared with United's best and worst ever managers, Don Revie and Dennis Wise. Grayson had also presided over 13 straight league wins at Elland Road, and one more would beat another Revie record. It may have been in the third tier of English football, but it was still an impressive feat. Grayson had turned our home into an impenetrable fortress within two weeks of taking over a beleaguered team.

Grayson wasn't having it all his own way though. For a start, Leeds weren't even top of the league – Charlton Athletic led the way with a superior goal difference. Then there were the injuries. Ben Parker had been cruelly injured just 15 minutes after creating the opening goal of the season; crueller still, it was the last time Grayson would be able to field his impressive young left-back for eight months. Captain Richard Naylor was yet to make an appearance due to his back injury, while his intended new centre-back partner, Patrick Kisnorbo, had suffered a serious head injury in the opening-day victory over Exeter, leaving a wound that required plastic surgery to fix. Desperate to secure his place in the team, Kisnorbo refused to have surgery, which would rule him out of action. Instead he wore a special bandage which would stem the flow of blood when the wound inevitably re-opened during battle. The process was repeating itself every match but even so, Kisnorbo happily played through the pain, endearing himself to the Leeds fans in heroic fashion.

Kisnorbo's warrior spirit wasn't the only reason Elland Road had a new hero. His performances were a revelation, the key component of a defence that had only conceded three goals in the early weeks of the season, and none from open play (two penalties and a direct free kick). Eyebrows had been raised when Grayson signed a player who had played only eight games in the previous 18 months due to two serious knee injuries, but as usual the manager's judgement was proving correct.

> *Jermaine Beckford: 'Paddy was brilliant, he was the leader everyone needs. When things were going well he'd keep you grounded, and when they weren't going well he'd pick you up. And if you'd been playing crap, you'd know about it very quickly!'*

Kisnorbo missed the visit of Stockport County due to international duty with Australia, and Grayson was also without Rui Marques, who had picked up an Achilles injury. Although it wasn't a serious problem, Leeds's longest-serving player had started his last league game for the club. He'd lost the trust of his manager and never got a chance to regain it. Instead, Grayson parted with an actual transfer fee to sign utility defender Leigh Bromby from Sheffield United. At £250,000, Bromby was one of the most expensive purchases of the League One era, and although he wasn't the most gifted footballer it was money well spent. Bromby's versatility made him the first person called upon when Crowe, Naylor, Kisnorbo or Hughes were unavailable, and only eight players would feature more than him this season. Like his manager and captain, it was an added bonus that Bromby was Leeds through and through, and another bonus was his killer long throw.

More concerning than a reshuffled defence was the absence of Beckford, who was bang in form with five goals in five games. Mike Grella was given the unenviable task of filling Beckford's boots but he passed the test with flying colours, opening the scoring inside the first ten minutes against Stockport. Grella's finish was lovely, curling the ball from the corner of the box perfectly inside the far post, but the goal owed much to the virtues of Leeds's young midfield trio. Howson's tenacity won the ball, Snodgrass's twinkle toes took him away from two defenders on the touchline, and Johnson's willingness to drive into the box paved the way for the American to bag his first goal in English football.

Ľubomír Michalík celebrated his first start of the season with a goal too, effectively putting the game to bed before half-time when prodding home a corner. Bromby could claim an assist to go with his debut clean sheet, having nipped in to head the ball practically (or literally) out of the goalkeeper's hands to set up the chance for his centre-back partner. Owain Fôn Williams was furious, but his protests only earned him a booking. 'TWO-NIL, IT'S YER KEEPER'S FAULT!' was the juvenile chant ringing around Elland Road, but Williams earned a second-half consolation by saving a weak Snodgrass penalty. It only served to keep the score respectable as a comeback was well beyond Stockport.

Jonny Howson: 'When you're one of the better teams in the league and confidence is high, you're going into every game expecting to get something, and it's very hard to stop.'

It hadn't been a vintage performance, but winning so comfortably with so many key absentees strengthened the belief that Leeds would be unstoppable in 2009/10. At the final whistle the Kop poured adulation on a record-breaking team they were proud to call their own, and their manager was a proud man too, 'There have been a lot of great players and teams here at Leeds, so for us to achieve these two records is fantastic. The players can be proud of what they have done.'

Leeds United 0 Liverpool 1

League Cup third round
Elland Road (38,168)

'These were the nights we were striving to get more regularly,
where everybody could show what good players they are, and
what a big football club this is.' – Simon Grayson

Ken Bates's latest attempt to create a mountain out of a molehill came when 16-year-old Luke Garbutt joined Everton from Leeds's Thorp Arch academy. Everton insisted they had done nothing wrong but, having lost a few academy prospects to Premier League clubs, Bates was keen to let his anger be known, 'The days of nicking Leeds players and paying peanuts are over. We are determined to be adequately compensated for the work we are doing in our academy.' His tirade did the trick; Everton were forced to pay three times the £200,000 they had initially offered for the England under-17 captain, with add-ons that would potentially take the fee up to £1.5m, plus a 20 per cent sell-on clause. Despite Garbutt spending 11 seasons at Goodison Park, not an extra penny was due to Leeds. Garbutt had more loan spells than appearances for Everton before he was finally released in 2020, with no sell-on fee for Leeds, no testimonial for his long service, and not so much as a farewell from his manager, Carlo Ancelotti, who didn't even know who he was.

Leeds's 100 per cent record came to an end on a Friday night trip to Southend, but they could still come away feeling pretty pleased with themselves after Shane Higgs saved a second-half penalty to earn a 0-0 draw. Anything was a bonus at Roots Hall. Leeds had visited four times in their history, scored one goal and never won. Normal service was resumed the following week with a 4-1 thrashing of Gillingham at Elland Road. Bradley Johnson continued his rich vein of form by scoring both first-half goals to take him on to five for the season, and not since the days of the great Gary Speed had Leeds had a midfielder who was so prolific in the air. Johnson possessed a similar spring and knack of timing that

The ever-humble Leeds fans after winning late at Tranmere

Howson's miracle moment

Prutton, Hughes and Ankergren: Wembley here we come!

The Globe

Me and Lewis

Wembley Way (left to right: Taylor, Cowling, Nige, George, Gianni, Fan, Paul, random stranger)

Hope and expectation

Atmosphere reaches fever pitch

*'Shit ground
no fans, shit
ground no fans'*

Total devastation

The Astonishing Fabien Delph

Becchio raises the roof before more play-off heartache

New season, new records

Beckford's perfect putt

All hands to the pump

You'll never beat Kisnorbo

The Hollywood Ending

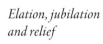

*Elation, jubilation
and relief*

Party Time

the legendary Welshman made his trademark, and he was proving to be a potent weapon for Grayson's team, not that he was getting carried away.

Bradley Johnson: 'I was having a competition with Becks for top goalscorer that season!'

Stand-in captain Jonny Howson made it 3-0 immediately after the restart with a classy goal that mirrored another legend from yesteryear, breaking from midfield like Lee Bowyer to take Beckford's flick on his chest before rifling low into the corner of the Kop net. Beckford rounded off the scoring himself in the closing stages (edging ahead of Johnson, six to five, in the scoring charts), but the biggest cheer of the day was reserved for the newly fixed big screen, when it showed that Norwich had held Charlton to a 2-2 draw. Grayson's men had finally reached the summit of League One, the first time Leeds had ever led the division (for longer than two hours). 'AND NOW YOU'RE GONNA BELIEVE US ... WE'RE GONNA WIN THE LEAGUE!'

Confidence on the terraces was sky-high, as it was within the team. Goals were coming from all areas and the defence was almost watertight – top spot was the least they deserved. But a more generous reward came from the League Cup third round draw, which gave Leeds the opportunity to take on old foes Liverpool.

Over 38,000 packed into Elland Road, and the old girl was bouncing all the way through a captivating tie as the Mighty Whites gave the Mighty Reds a mighty scare. Rafa Benítez had come tantalisingly close to breaking Liverpool's 20-year wait for a league title in the previous season, and even in making nine changes he still fielded a full team of internationals, with six more internationals on the bench. Jamie Carragher and Javier Mascherano were the players who retained their places, with Benítez wary of keeping a solid and experienced, world-class spine. It was enough to get through, but it might not have been.

> *Simon Grayson: 'The club had been waiting a number of years to play a top Premier League club. The atmosphere was amazing and we gave them a real good run for their money. Snodgrass had [Andrea] Dossena on toast in the first half, he didn't know which way he was going, left or right. Maybe Snoddy didn't even know which way he was going, but he was unplayable! It was a great experience for all the players.'*

Straight from the off, the League One side attacked fearlessly. Doyle missed the target with a six-yard free header, then Beckford had a goal wrongly ruled out for offside when he stabbed home Michalík's downward header. He was clearly onside, so perhaps the flag was raised against Luciano Becchio, who tried to steal the goal on the line from an offside position (whether he did or not was a tighter call than on Beckford). Before the game I would have been thrilled to be heading into the second half attacking the Kop at 0-0, but when the half-time whistle blew it was a great frustration that Leeds weren't already ahead. In the second half Beckford could have made up for the misfortune of his disallowed goal when he raced on to a long clearance ahead of a hesitant defence, but the ball was bouncing unkindly and Beckford's shot was tame and straight at the goalkeeper.

Nobody could argue that Leeds did not at least match their illustrious opponents, but the only goal of the game was scored by David N'Gog of Liverpool, who applied a quality finish when afforded half a yard to shuffle and shoot inside the box. Glen Johnson, Steven Gerrard and Martin Škrtel were all called from the bench to ensure Liverpool ground out a victory that Benítez described as 'fantastic', while

Grayson was left proud as a peacock and felt his team had deserved to win.

What a thrill it was to experience a night of scintillating football between two giants of the English game. It whetted the appetite and made everybody at the club that bit more determined to bring the good times back, and reminded the country what they were missing too. There aren't many better places to watch a football match than at a rocking Elland Road.

——

Milton Keynes Dons 0 Leeds United 1

Matchday 9 of 46
Stadium: MK (16,713)

> *'It was a great way to finish a game, celebrating the goal and a valuable three points right in front of the away end.'*
> *– Simon Grayson*

Four days after the Lord Mayor's Show against Liverpool, Leeds headed to Milton Keynes. I am naturally a pessimistic Leeds fan (most of us are), but sometimes I get pangs of certainty that go beyond the normal feelings of expecting the worst. Travelling down to Milton Keynes was one such occasion. My main reason for expecting nothing but defeat was because of the effort put in against Liverpool, and how often teams come 'crashing down to earth' after such a big occasion. Plus, Milton Keynes were a very dangerous side, considered one of the favourites for promotion this season. Paul Ince had taken over from Roberto Di Matteo in the summer and I knew he would have his team fired up in anticipation of a barrage of abuse from the Leeds fans, who still hadn't forgiven him for playing for Manchester United in the early 1990s.

MK Dons had finished third in 2008/09 and lost in the play-off semi-finals to Scunthorpe, but they had recovered well and had only lost once, trailing table-topping, record-breaking Leeds by five points. Aaron Wilbraham, Jason Puncheon and another former Red Devil, Luke Chadwick, formed a dangerous three-pronged attack, and within a minute Wilbraham had the first opportunity of the game but fired straight at Shane Higgs. A difficult start became more challenging when Jason Crowe hobbled off injured after just eight minutes, and with Bromby filling in at right-back Leeds lost some of their threat down the right. Having already started the game without half of their potent strike force (Becchio had failed a late fitness test) it wasn't particularly surprising or too disappointing to watch a first half devoid of goalmouth action but right on half-time, having just forced a decent save from Higgs, Puncheon flew into a tackle on Michael Doyle which drew a straight red card from referee Andy D'Urso. What a boost!

Keen to take full advantage of the opportunity presented to him, and without a natural full-back in the squad anyway, Grayson swapped Andy Hughes for Andy Robinson and effectively changed to a 3-3-4 formation. It didn't really click, and with Leeds struggling to penetrate the deep-lying defence, it was fortunate that Grayson didn't make a third and final substitution before his goalkeeper picked up an injury and was forced off. With Ankergren introduced for the final 30 minutes Grayson had no more cards to play, and just like the first half, the second was drifting towards a drab goalless finish, until Leeds won a 92nd-minute free kick near the corner flag in front of us.

For the life of me I cannot understand what happened next. In Robert Snodgrass, Leeds had one of the best set-piece takers in the division (if not the country, in my over-zealous opinion), and in Bradley Johnson they had one of the most dangerous aerial threats, but for some reason Johnson was trusted with delivering the last chance of the game and Snodgrass was sent into the box (both were left-footed too, so this wasn't a case of in-swinger versus out-swinger). They had combined for three set-piece goals already this season and they did so again, with Snoddy meeting Johnson's near-post delivery and steering his header beyond a helpless goalkeeper.

> *Bradley Johnson: 'Snoddy scored a header?! You'll have to send me the video of that!'*

All last-minute winners are special, but the extra anticipation when they come from set pieces makes them all the more dramatic, sweeter too, when scored in front of a 5,000-strong travelling army. The players went as crazy as the fans, every one of them huddling in the technical area with the substitutes and the coaches. What a sight! Grayson remembers the moment well, but could only speculate about how the match-winning combination came about.

> *Simon Grayson: 'I've not got a clue! Snodgrass was probably knackered and couldn't be arsed walking across to take the free kick because he was playing on the right-hand side. Bradley was already on the left so decided to swing it in and it's just hit Snoddy's head and gone in!'*

Leeds had snatched a huge three points, 'the type of victory that gets you out of this league', according to the *Yorkshire Evening Post*'s Phil Hay. Me and Paul were on cloud nine walking back to the car, so much so that our spirits were barely dampened when we discovered a parking ticket on my windscreen. I'd worried that the parking spot had been too good to be true, but with other cars mounted on the grass verge near the ground I just assumed everyone else knew best. We were so cock-a-hoop with the late win that we took the ticket as a positive – £30 for a kick-ass parking spot, that's only £15 each! Also, with us making an onward journey to London, we surmised that we now had a pass to park anywhere we wanted for free: if we already had a ticket on the windscreen we wouldn't get another, would we? By the time we arrived in London the adrenaline had subsided enough for us to bottle testing out the theory, but it was never going to ruin the night, Leeds were top of the league and looking unstoppable!

——

Leeds United 2 Norwich City 1
Matchday 12 of 46
Elland Road (19,912)

> *'The last-minute winner, it just means that much more. There's more of a buzz.'* – Jonny Howson

After the highs of the Liverpool and MK Dons games, perhaps it should have come as no great surprise that Leeds suffered their first disappointing result of the season, dropping two points at home to Carlisle on a Tuesday night. The 75th-minute equaliser was only the fifth goal Leeds had conceded all season and ended their record-breaking 15-match winning streak in the league at Elland Road. Grayson admitted afterwards that his team had deserved nothing more.

Despite setting League One alight, and the relentless run of home wins, Leeds's attendances were still on the decline. The Carlisle match attracted a season's low of just 19,000, but five days later there were over 30,000 in the ground for a top-of-the-table clash with Charlton. Typically, the bumper crowd were subjected to a dour stalemate, although Grayson was pleased with another clean sheet and pleased to be heading into the international break as undefeated league leaders.

There was more good news for the city during the international break as Leeds Rhinos won their third successive

Super League Grand Final, the first team to do so, with St Helens on the losing end yet again. However, at Elland Road there was more unrest. Ken Bates delivered yet another slap in the fans' faces by failing to take up an option to purchase the Thorp Arch training ground, which had been sold to keep the club afloat after relegation from the Premier League. The cost of the annual lease was £486,000, and would increase by three per cent every year, but Leeds had a buy-back option for the modest price of £6m, which expired on 16 October 2009. Having sold Fabian Delph for £6m the fans naively thought the money would be used to reclaim Thorp Arch (which would have been a poetic tribute to Delph's legacy), but our miserly chairman would only do a deal with the help of the local council, and with no deal struck by the time the deadline passed, the club was saddled with extortionate lease payments for the next 20 years. Cheers, Ken!

> *Simon Grayson: 'It's never an ideal situation when the fans are at loggerheads with the owner. He had his faults, but I had a good day-to-day relationship with Bates. He liked my sense of humour and I'd sometimes take the mickey out of him, but ultimately, I was very respectful towards him as the owner of the club. And I'll be eternally grateful that he fulfilled a dream of mine by giving me the opportunity to manage Leeds United.'*

'Cuddly Ken' was a shrewd operator and attempted to appease the fans in the only way he knew how, by dipping into the emergency loan market. On the day of the Norwich match, televised live on *Monday Night Football*, Leeds completed two emergency loan signings – and for a change they were genuinely exciting arrivals. Sam Vokes was a 19-year-old Welsh international striker for Premier League Wolves, who had been their first reserve during promotion from the

Championship in the previous season, scoring seven goals. His game time was limited in the Premier League so he arrived at Leeds looking to gain experience and provide genuine competition for Becchio and Beckford. Joining him at Elland Road was a 21-year-old Ivorian winger, Max Gradel, who had been a prominent feature in Leicester's League One-winning team in 2009 but hadn't made a single appearance in the Championship. With fixtures coming thick and fast in the FA Cup and Football League Trophy, this appeared to be an excellent double swoop.

> *Jonny Howson: 'There are certain players I've always thought I'd love to be able to play with again, and Max is certainly one of them. Off the pitch he was a great guy – full of energy, full of life – and it's enjoyable to have people like that in your squad and around the place. Like with Snoddy, he could get a bit upset, a bit angry, but that's just character and passion, because he wants to do well. And what a player he was too.'*

The novelty of being live on Sky must have affected the attendance for the Norwich match, which again dropped below 20,000. This brought rise to a new chant that would become a regular for a decade and beyond, in which Elland Road declares what it thinks of Sky TV. With Becchio still missing, Vokes was thrown straight into the team – an early birthday present on his last day as a teenager – while Gradel was immediately put on the bench with Grayson's patience with Andy Robinson seemingly expired. Norwich had recovered well from their disastrous start and were already in the play-off zone when their game in hand kicked off at Elland Road. They were looking to close the gap on Leeds to five points and a bright opening had the Whites chasing shadows, yet it was the home side who took the lead courtesy of a Bradley Johnson header from a Snodgrass corner – normal service resumed.

Norwich deservedly levelled when Grant Holt got the wrong side of his marker to convert at the Kop end just before half-time, and the second half seemed to be drifting towards a 1-1 draw that would keep comfortable daylight between the sides. But Leeds needed a win to return to the top of the league, so Grayson threw on Trésor Kandol and Gradel for the final ten minutes in an attempt to turn the screw. It worked a treat. Gradel was a livewire straight away, fast as lightning with quick feet to match, and he looked the part too with a strip of peroxide hair on top of his head, a sure sign of his confidence. The substitutions helped Leeds to grab the initiative, and Kandol and Gradel combined to set up Beckford with a huge chance to win the game, but Fraser Forster made a terrific block. In the dying seconds Gradel's pace got him in behind the full-back and should have led to the winning goal but Beckford, sliding in, couldn't quite get enough on the ball which flashed wide of the post. There were gasps all around Elland Road; the chance to steal another epic win had gone.

Jermaine Beckford: 'Whenever I played I knew I'd get chances galore due to my movement and my team-mates, so I was never too worried about missing chances because I knew I'd get another. When I slid that chance wide I remember looking at the scoreboard and seeing 90 minutes, and thinking there must be time for one more chance.'

I expected the resulting goal kick to bring the final whistle, but Forster stubbed his toe as he cleared upfield, and with the Norwich defenders on their heels, Beckford latched on to the loose ball, sprinted clear, and found the back of the net, perhaps with a little help from the boot of a desperate covering defender. Elland Road exploded with joy, and fans from the Kop spilled on to the pitch as players and supporters formed a mass huddle by the corner flag around the match-winner. They were such joyous scenes, it was as if Leeds had secured promotion already. But that's how it felt, such was the momentum behind Grayson's team. Leeds were back on top of League One, now 11 points clear of a Norwich side whose form, and performance at Elland Road, suggested they would be one of the top teams in the league.

In a carbon copy of their first season in League One, Leeds were still unbeaten heading into a matchday 13 visit to Millwall, a fixture that often seemed to be the litmus test for a Whites side. After their epic semi-final victory at Elland Road the Lions had lost at Wembley to Scunthorpe, and with only four victories in the new season they were struggling to overcome the heartbreak of a play-off final defeat, a common phenomenon in football. But not as common as a team being galvanised by hosting Leeds, and Millwall duly ground out a hard-fought 2-1 victory.

Dennis Wise's team had overcome the hurdle of Millwall away on matchday 13, but where Wise's men began to struggle after their trip to The Den, Grayson's players responded in spectacular fashion. A long midweek trip to Bristol Rovers wasn't the kindest fixture to follow a bruising defeat, but Leeds dismantled the hosts with ease. A clean sheet and goals for your strikers is always the perfect combination, and accompanying this clean sheet was a beautiful Beckford brace, a first goal for Vokes, and a goal too for the resurgent Kandol.

At the weekend Leeds made it successive 4-0 victories, against a Yeovil side unbeaten in six and high on confidence. The Whites were already ahead when Gradel entered the fray on the hour, but it was his introduction that sparked a previously subdued performance into life. Within ten minutes Gradel had bagged his first goal for the club, skipping inside his marker before firing a low left-footed drive into the far corner of the Kop net. 'GRAYSON, GRAYSON SIGN HIM UP!' chanted the Kop. The Elland Road faithful had only seen

Gradel play 20 minutes over two matches, but their verdict was unanimous.

It was almost a hat-trick of 4-0 wins, but Leeds had to settle for 3-0 at the Withdean Stadium, a result that ruined Gus Poyet's first home game in charge of Brighton & Hove Albion. For the fans it was a little bit of revenge for Poyet's abrupt Elland Road departure that derailed the 2007/08 season, though Grayson's extra satisfaction will have come from his reshuffled midfield. This was the first time he hadn't been able to field his favoured quartet of Snodgrass, Howson, Doyle and Johnson, but Neil Kilkenny proved to be a superb addition, giving Leeds greater control in midfield. The Australian set up the first two goals with raking crossfield passes, and popped up with a late goal himself.

Leeds were absolutely flying now. They'd played a game less than their promotion rivals but had built a six-point lead at the top, and a nine-point lead over third-placed Huddersfield Town, with the West Yorkshire derby on the horizon.

—

Leeds United 2 Huddersfield Town 2
Matchday 19 of 46
Elland Road (36,723)

'My assistant, Ian Miller, said Gradel was like a bottle of pop. You shake him up and open it up, and it just goes everywhere! That was Max to a tee. We just knew he'd thrive at a big club like Leeds.' – Simon Grayson

Midweek games at Elland Road always made life difficult for me, because my dad's snooker team, Birstwith B, also played on a Tuesday night and I was their best player. I was pretty good at snooker, I even once made a century break, although my 101 came in practice against myself, with only God as my witness. Me and my dad were hell-bent on winning the snooker league, and finishing runners-up on three occasions fuelled the fire as we chased Birstwith's first title since 1982, the year before I was born.

My passion to bring home the championship was reflected by my willingness to miss midweek away games, and for Tuesday night home fixtures I would rush back after the full-time whistle to play in the fifth and final frame of the match, with my dad playing the fourth frame at a snail's pace to ensure I arrived on time. Once a season, on Cup Finals Night, this wouldn't be possible as the format required a full night of doubles play, and the 2009 Nidderdale Cup clashed with Leyton Orient at home. Knowing we had a great chance of winning our first trophy, I sacrificed Elland Road, for which I was kindly rewarded.

Rather than playing in a tiny village hall (some of which didn't have sufficient room around the table to cue properly, others with such inadequate heating that condensation would cover the baize during the winter months), Cup Finals Night was played at the Manhattan Snooker Club in Harrogate, and between frames I was able to nip to the bar to check the Leeds score on Sky Sports News. Each time I did it remained 0-0, but at 9.30pm, just before the final cued off, a disappointing draw turned into another thrilling win thanks to the man of the moment, Max Gradel. I was disappointed to have missed the Elland Road Shuffle – even more so when I saw the goal, a piece of individual magic with Gradel twisting and turning on the edge of the box before drilling into the roof of the Kop net – but I was delighted with the win, and completed a terrific night's work by winning the final and delivering Birstwith's first trophy in 27 years.

Leeds had played five cup ties in the six weeks since defeat at Millwall, so Grayson fielded a much-changed team for the next league fixture, a midweek trip to Oldham, where Leeds's travelling army outnumbered the home fans in an attendance of 7,793. Beckford, Becchio and Snodgrass were all left on the bench, and Michael Doyle was rested altogether despite the defence already being significantly weakened by injuries to Naylor and Kisnorbo, and of course the long-term absentee, Ben Parker. Goalkeeper Shane Higgs was still injured too, although Casper Ankergren's performances suggested he may have regained his number one status regardless.

Into the side came David Prutton, making his first league start of the season, as did two new loan signings, left-back Tony Capaldi and striker Hogan Ephraim. It was a brave selection from Grayson and it paid off. Super-subs often underwhelm when finally given a start, but Gradel was the match-winner again with both assists as Leeds racked up their fifth successive victory and clean sheet. For Prutton, it would prove to be his last start for the club.

> David Prutton: 'Given my age and the stage of my career, I was chewing not to be playing. But I understood it – if I'm playing wide and you have the option of a Robert Snodgrass, it's a no-brainer, you play Snodgrass every time. There's a key period where you think you have time to work your way back into the team, but as time passes you realise you have to take responsibility for your own career. If I couldn't play at Leeds I'd have to find somewhere else to play, which was sad, but it's the way it is.'

With 45 points from the first 18 games, the Whites were looking unstoppable. They held a six-point lead at the top and a ten-point lead over third-placed Norwich, and had a game in hand on all their rivals. It was starting to look like an unassailable position, even to the most pessimistic of Leeds fans.

Next up was the West Yorkshire derby with Huddersfield, in front of League One's biggest crowd of the season by far.

The big guns returned to the team, and it was back to 'impact sub' duty for the red-hot Gradel. His loan deal only had a month to run, and it came as no surprise that Grayson was desperate to keep hold of the ace up his sleeve.

Simon Grayson: 'Max was a fantastic lad to work with. A lovely kid, hard-working, with enough ability to add to the strong squad we already had. He gave us an extra impetus.'

Unfortunately, Gradel's form wasn't going unnoticed at his parent club and Leicester manager Nigel Pearson ruled out any permanent move, saying, 'He's not for sale. It's as simple as that.' If there was any chance of keeping Gradel he would have to rein in his irrepressible form, but the Ivorian further dented his chances of staying at Elland Road with another marvellous cameo against Huddersfield.

On derby day in 2008/09 it had taken Robert Snodgrass just three minutes to open the scoring, and a year later it took him just two thanks to yet another Elland Road howler from Alex Smithies. The ball was like a wet bar of soap to the young goalkeeper, who spilled a shot then let it squirm loose out of his hands as he pounced on it, allowing Snodgrass to give the hosts the perfect start. The carbon copy of the previous season continued when Huddersfield deservedly equalised early in the second half, but just when the Terriers' tails were wagging Leeds hit them with a sucker punch.

Gradel had been on the pitch for two minutes when a Huddersfield corner brought a great save from Ankergren, who then delivered an even greater punt downfield that bounced all the way through to the opposite penalty area. Beckford was chasing and jumped with Smithies, beating the keeper to the ball, and with both players in a heap on the floor Gradel pounced, touched it past the stranded Terrier and fired unstoppably past the defenders on the line, low into the corner. Elland Road went bonkers as Gradel bounced for joy by the corner flag – what an exhilarating goal!

Gradel had stolen the headlines but the plaudits went to Ankergren for his save and subsequent quick thinking that led to the goal. The Dane had returned to the team when Higgs suffered a recurrence of his injury during the Norwich match, and leading into the derby he had kept five successive clean sheets in the league. I knew Leeds were lucky to have a goalkeeper of Ankergren's class at the club, luckier still that he'd stuck around despite Grayson bringing in a new number one in the summer, but I hadn't realised his Elland Road career would have been over but for the misfortune of his team-mate.

Casper Ankergren: 'Shane had done really well in the friendlies and I had no problem with him starting the season. Then he got injured and I came in for three games, but after just one training session Shane was back in the team for the Norwich game. I was really angry with that. I called a meeting with Grayson the next day and told him it was no problem if he didn't fancy me, I would go somewhere else. But Shane had got injured 16 minutes into the Norwich game, and I think Grayson probably knew how long he would be out for and told me he really liked me and wanted me to stay.'

As the season developed we would feel more and more fortunate that Ankergren didn't take the pig-headed approach and demand to leave regardless of Higgs's injury, but on this day there was nothing he could do to prevent Huddersfield from spoiling the party when Jordan Rhodes equalised ten minutes after Gradel's goal, earning the visitors a deserved share of the points.

It had been a great derby, and despite the frustration of dropping two points it felt a treat to have experienced such a riveting game of football, the type seldom seen in the third tier. The performance had been slightly disappointing though, with Leeds not appearing any fresher despite the rests afforded to key players in midweek. Perhaps they were distracted, as in three days' time they faced an FA Cup second round replay with Kettering Town, a match that had obtained all the importance of a semi-final.

—

Leeds United 5 Kettering Town 1

FA Cup second round replay
Elland Road (10,670)

> 'Going into extra time the tie was on a knife edge. You know that one mistake could cost you the chance to go to Old Trafford.' – Simon Grayson

Leeds were heading for another embarrassing FA Cup defeat to non-league opposition until Jermaine Beckford spared their blushes with a late equaliser at Kettering Town, which secured a replay and a place in the hat for the third round draw. The match had been televised on the Sunday afternoon and the draw immediately followed. I loved cup draws, they always enthralled me and kept me on the edge of my seat until Leeds came out, even in the days when they had no chance of winning the competition. The excitement was all in the moment, what fixture would we get?

Tottenham were the first to be drawn and the excitement levels were instantly raised. I loved White Hart Lane, going back would be mouthwatering, but next out were Peterborough. Sigh. At least we couldn't get Peterborough so one crap draw was out of the picture. Next out of the hat were Brentford, raising my anxiety levels. What a terrible draw that would be, please don't let it be Leeds! The balls were numbered alphabetically (Arsenal would be number one) so the low ball drawn next brought a sigh of relief even before it was revealed as Doncaster Rovers. Next out was a mid-range ball, were Leeds at home? No, it was Middlesbrough, which wouldn't be a bad draw, local rival and all, but the next pick was Manchester City.

While I didn't know exactly what number Leeds were, the broadcasters had introduced a new feature, listing the names and numbers of the remaining big clubs down the side of the screen. I really didn't like this as it removed the moment of uncertain drama as you wait to hear which team goes with the drawn number; instead your eye instinctively darts to the list, searching for the answer a millisecond sooner. However, this new feature eventually added to the drama, because as the draw progressed and Leeds remained, seeing the list of clubs we could still face was stoking the excitement levels. Eventually, there were so few teams remaining that Leeds joined the list on the side of the screen, and then the list started getting shorter. We were at the business end.

With ten teams left to draw, both Leeds and their bitterest rivals, Manchester United, remained. Newcastle were there too, along with Bolton and Leicester who would both be decent away draws, but there was only one prize we wanted now. With a realistic chance of drawing Manchester United, every pick was terrifying. Plymouth Argyle came out next but were followed by Newcastle. Phew! Leicester City, followed by Swansea. Get in! With just six balls remaining the dream draw was now a serious possibility. 'Bolton Wanderers will play Lincoln City.' COME ON! Paul and I were on our feet, yelling with excitement.

Noel Edmonds's game show *Deal or No Deal* was the most popular thing on daytime TV, and Leeds found themselves in an equivalent position to the game's most dramatic climax. With only four teams left the £250,000 box was still in the game (Manchester United), but so too was the 1p (Accrington

Stanley), and the 10p (Gillingham). The next ball drawn was now irrelevant, whoever it was, Leeds had a 2/1 chance of drawing their arch enemy. It was Accrington Stanley, and Paul and I held our breath, clasped our hands together, and prayed for the next ball to be Gillingham. 'GILLINGHAM! FUCKING GET IN!' With only Leeds and Manchester United remaining in the hat we were already dancing around the lounge in jubilation, but the next ball drawn brought a second wave of ecstatic cheers. It was Man United: we were going to Old Trafford!

What a roller coaster, it was like a cup run itself and we had landed the dream draw! Unless there had been some cock-up and the last ball wasn't Leeds, but that would be too far-fetched even for a cursed club like ours, and Leeds were indeed the last ball out of the hat. Well, Leeds or Kettering.

Despite the prize on offer, the crowd for the replay with Kettering was shockingly low. Just 10,000 turned up at Elland Road and I was one of the many thousand absentees who were rightly scorned by the fans in attendance. Grayson picked a full-strength team, not taking any chances of missing out on a shot at the Premier League champions, and the players were taking it as seriously as their manager, tearing through their non-league opponents almost at will. Luciano Becchio opened the scoring after 20 minutes, which by then was a great relief as it had already started to feel like it could be 'one of those nights', with Leeds missing chance after chance in the opening stages. At half-time it was still only 1-0, but I felt calm, there was only one team in this match. However, football is rarely that straightforward, especially when United are involved, and Kettering came out fighting in the second half.

Cometh the hour, cometh the man. It was less than two years since Anthony Elding signed for Leeds, but after one goal in ten poor games he was sold to Crewe Alexandra. After one league goal in 26 games for Crewe, Elding had been frozen out again, and now on loan at Kettering he rocked Elland Road with an unlikely equaliser, putting our dream trip to Old Trafford in serious jeopardy. The Whites were now awash with nerves, with only Neil Kilkenny seeming to keep his composure. The little Australian was dictating the game superbly in midfield but his team-mates weren't doing anything to help him, and as the game drifted towards extra time the last big chance fell to substitute Trésor Kandol, who was denied by a goal-line clearance. Extra time it would be.

I was beyond agitated now, surely we weren't going to blow this opportunity? No sooner had extra time got under way than Snodgrass hit the post. It felt like Leeds had hit the woodwork a dozen times, but it was probably more like half a dozen. At half-time it was still 1-1 and we were 15 minutes away from the jeopardy of penalties. Supporting England, Italy and Leeds through the 1990s, I had seen my teams win once out of eight penalty shoot-outs, and my record in this decade wasn't much better, so now I was terrified.

With a last throw of the dice Grayson introduced Mike Grella, and two minutes later the American scored a beautiful goal to nudge Leeds ahead. I had only just finished jumping around the living room when Kandol doubled the lead; Leeds were practically there, what a relief! Five minutes later the result was put beyond any doubt when Grella added his second, and in the 119th minute, with Leeds's 42nd attempt at goal, Jermaine Beckford made it 5-1. There was still time for Grella to miss the chance for a hat-trick and for Beckford to strike the post, but it mattered not. Leeds were heading to Old Trafford!

Bradley Johnson: 'I hadn't realised the size of the rivalry between Leeds and Man U. When we knew we were going to play them the atmosphere of the whole city changed. Everyone was counting down to that match, but Simon

*would never let us look beyond the next game. We had to get
on with the job and keep performing in the league.'*

———

Leeds United 1 Southampton 0

Matchday 21 of 46
Elland Road (25,948)

*'I took him off and he wasn't happy, he had a bit of a sulk. No
individual is bigger than the club.' – Simon Grayson*

After such an energy-sapping midweek game it was no bad
result when Leeds were held to a goalless draw at Brentford
at the weekend. They could have won it, but young Polish
goalkeeper Wojciech Szczęsny denied Beckford with a
stunning save, somehow tipping his blistering volley against
the post. The successive draws had enabled Charlton to move
within striking distance of Leeds, the Londoners now only
two points behind and hoping to steal the Christmas number
one spot in the last round of matches before the turkeys were
cooked.

United's opponents were Southampton, newly relegated
from the Championship and restricted by a ten-point deduction
for going into administration. The now debt-free club were
ambitious, and their high-profile manager, Alan Pardew, was
still targeting promotion; after all, he had one of the strongest
squads in the division. They had spent £3m on rebuilding,
with Rickie Lambert alone costing similar to what Leeds had
spent in total during their three seasons in League One. His
partner up front, David Connolly, had 41 Republic of Ireland
caps to his name, and feeding them from midfield were young
starlets Adam Lallana and Morgan Schneiderlin. This was as
tough an opponent as the Whites would face in League One.
Things hadn't gelled immediately for Pardew. It had taken

Southampton eight games to register their first win but they were now on a roll with four successive victories (and one defeat in 11) bringing them within nine points of the play-off zone.

After plenty of tinkering in recent weeks, Grayson's team had a familiar look about it for this game. Naylor and Kisnorbo were reunited in defence, as were Becchio and Beckford in attack, but in the middle of the park Neil Kilkenny's form had rendered him undroppable. Consequently, Jonny Howson was shunted to a right-sided midfield role with creator extraordinaire Robert Snodgrass moved to the left, consigning Bradley Johnson and his seven goals from midfield to the bench, along with the explosive impact-sub, Max Gradel.

A healthy pre-Christmas crowd was treated to a great game which Leeds dominated thanks to one of their best performances of the season. Naylor and Kisnorbo suffocated any Southampton attacks before they became dangerous, while at the other end only wastefulness by Becchio and Beckford prevented a greater margin of victory. Beckford especially was having a torrid afternoon, so much so that the 15-goal hitman was withdrawn with 15 minutes to go, initiating a memorable couple of minutes.

By now I absolutely loved Grayson; he was my favourite Leeds manager of all time. He was doing a fantastic job, he said the right things at the right time, and he clearly loved Leeds United as much as the fans. But my favourite thing about him was his knack of making the exact substitutions I wanted! On this occasion I was desperate for Grayson to replace Beckford, who was having a real off-day. I never really expected our talisman to be withdrawn though, so when Beckford's number went up so too did my love for the manager. But Beckford stood motionless in the middle of the pitch, his disbelief verging on protestation. Time was running out and Leeds were pushing for a winner, and Beckford almost had to be goaded off the pitch. When he eventually reached the dugout he rejected Grayson's outstretched hand.

Jermaine Beckford: 'There was no malice, just pure frustration at not being able to play well, score a goal, or help win the game. When you're playing you're young, full of testosterone and playing on edge, and, to me, seeing my number come up made me feel like a failure. It's the wrong mindset, but that's how I felt.'

The incident had stoked the atmosphere, and two minutes later came the crescendo when Robert Snodgrass picked the ball up on the edge of the Southampton box, dribbled past a defender and, with his weaker right foot, curled the ball exquisitely into the top corner. Me and Paul were sent tumbling down the gangway in jubilation, and when we recovered our composure it was time to pay homage, but it wasn't Snodgrass's name ringing around Elland Road. Instead, it was the most raucous chanting of a manager's name since we were calling Dennis Wise a w*nker, 'ONE SIMON GRAYSON! THERE'S ONLY ONE SIMON GRAYSON! ONE SIMON GRAAAAAYSON! THERE'S ONLY ONE SIMON GRAYSON!'

I screamed the words as loud as I could. I was so hurt for him, so pleased for him and so proud of him all at the same time, and proud of our fans for backing the manager over the star player.

Simon Grayson: 'You make decisions and they aren't always the right ones, but we scored straight away and the chant for me went round the ground. I'd forgotten about that!'

Leeds saw out the victory, extending their lead at the top after Charlton drew 4-4 with Millwall, but all the questions after the match were understandably about Beckford. Grayson pulled no punches, 'Obviously Jermaine is disappointed to be substituted, and I'm disappointed with his reaction.'

Within days it was water under the bridge. Beckford apologised to his manager and was back in the team and back in the goals for the Boxing Day fixture at home to Hartlepool, bagging a brace in a 3-1 victory. Beckford scored twice again two days later as Leeds inflicted an 11th straight defeat on Stockport County. The 4-2 scoreline may sound resounding, but United had trailed 2-1 in the second half and only took the lead in the 87th minute thanks to Leigh Bromby's first goal for the club, before Beckford added the icing to the cake.

It was another match that left me thinking there was no way this team wasn't going to win the league, but Leeds weren't resting on their laurels and on the eve of the transfer window opening they rejected a £1.25m bid from Newcastle for Beckford. It was a sizeable offer for a League One player with six months left on his contract but, reassuringly, Bates wasn't willing to upset the apple cart. His manager was a relieved man.

> *Simon Grayson: 'I just didn't feel the money Newcastle were offering weighed up against the bigger picture of getting the club back into the Championship. And fair play to Ken Bates, he backed me on that decision.'*

At the halfway point of the season Leeds were eight points clear at the top, with a game in hand, and on course to reach 112 points by the end. They had only lost once in the league all season, were banging in goals for fun and rock-solid at the back. There could be no better time to head to Old Trafford, to take on the biggest challenge in English football.

———

Manchester United 0 Leeds United 1
FA Cup third round
Old Trafford (74,526)

> *'One season losing to Histon in the cup, the season after beating Man U away in the cup. That's just Leeds United, isn't it!'* – Jonny Howson

On Saturday, 21 October 2000, my dad offered me a £50 bet that Leeds would win at Old Trafford in the next ten years. I snapped his hand off. We were on our way back from a 3-0 defeat at the home of the enemy, on a day where everything that could go wrong did go wrong. In my head they were too lucky and we were too unlucky to ever get the better of them. My dad was very confident about winning the bet. Leeds hadn't won at Old Trafford since 1981 and the law of averages dictated that the barren run would come to an end soon, especially with the Whites primed for a decade of glory under David O'Leary.

Eight years later, with Leeds still in League One and not able to return to the Premier League in time to win my dad the bet, we agreed an early settlement, dad covering my £30 membership fee for the Birstwith Snooker Club. The spirit of the bet had been brought into disrepute by Leeds's collapse, so a reduced settlement seemed a fair outcome. When Leeds drew Manchester United in the 2010 FA Cup it was the very last chance for the clubs to meet before the ten years were up, quite the coincidence, and a fitting introduction to an astonishing match.

> *Jermaine Beckford: 'I used to go into town the night before a game, and the vibe before the Man United game was completely different. It went from a cheery, "Hey Becks, go grab yourself a goal tomorrow!" to a far more serious, "Becks, now don't you let us down tomorrow, this is the big one." So you knew what it meant to the fans.'*

'Ankergren, Crowe, Hughes, Naylor, Kisnorbo, Howson, Kilkenny, Doyle, Snodgrass, Becchio and Beckford: Go out

there and immortalise yourselves!' It became my favourite
Facebook post of all time, but sadly I got the team wrong,
with Bradley Johnson given the nod ahead of Snodgrass.

> *Simon Grayson: 'We more or less approached it like any
> game, but we knew we would need to be more solid and,
> being naturally central midfielders, Johnson and Howson
> could tuck in from the wide positions and make it a compact
> midfield. The full-backs had to be wary not to leave ourselves
> exposed at the back and Luciano dropped a little bit deeper,
> with Beckford on the shoulder, ready to run the channels and
> hit them on the counter-attack.'*

I drove to Manchester on Sunday morning with three friends,
yet none of us would watch the game together. Paul's ticket
was in the top tier behind the goal, in the extended allocation
always given to away fans in the FA Cup. I was in the normal
away corner, 'Scum Ron' (as he was known on my phone) was
in the Stretford End, and although Lewis was in the same
corner as me, he went to meet his other friends pre-match and
we never saw each other in the ground. It was fantastic being
back at Old Trafford, and such a vast contrast to the away
grounds we'd become accustomed to visiting. Stood next to
me was a young lad who wasn't old enough to remember the
Premier League days; for him it must have been surreal.

I was nervous, apprehensive, but also so excited, and in the
back of my mind I wondered whether there was at least the
slightest chance of an upset. After all, there hadn't been one
in round three yet, and there always has to be at least one. I
had brashly prophesied to my Manchester United-supporting
friends that Ferguson's reserves would have their Old Trafford
careers ended by Leeds, but the team news made mission
impossible seem impossible. As the names of the home team
were read out in numerical order I was trying to scramble

together their formation in my head, but after six names I gave up. 'Number two, Gary Neville. Number six, Wes Brown. Number eight, Anderson. Number nine, Dimitar Berbatov. Number ten, Wayne Rooney. Number 15, Nemanja Vidić.' Oh shit!

With kick-off approaching the teams were read out for a second time, and the reality wasn't quite as bad as I had initially feared. They may have boasted a £60m front two, but the midfield quartet of Gabriel Obertan, Darron Gibson, Anderson and Danny Welbeck had an average age of just 21, while in defence, Vidić had picked up an injury in the warm-up, meaning a birthday surprise for Jonny Evans – 22 on the day and thrust into the starting 11. With 800 Manchester United appearances between them, Gary Neville and Wes Brown brought experience to the defence, but with Tomasz Kuszczak covering injured goalkeeper Edwin van der Sar it was a weaker team than Ferguson would have wanted to field. He must have thought his first-choice strike force would be enough to overwhelm League One Leeds, but if he did he thought wrong.

The opening 11 seconds set the tone for an unforgettable 90 minutes. The champions of England got us under way with a hopeful punt out to the wing looking for Welbeck, which landed straight on the head of Jason Crowe. It was a complacent, unimaginative, and poorly executed start, and the League One side's first taste of possession was the polar opposite; they swept up the pitch with lovely, inventive, one-touch passing, until Beckford's flashy attempt at taking the ball in his stride went wrong and it rolled out for a throw-in, to the ironic cheers of the home fans. Yet this was the first sign that Leeds would not be overawed on the big stage, and it felt very uplifting. A minute later, Gibson's shot from 35 yards was hit well enough to raise anxiety, but the ball flashed past the post. 'UNITED! UNITED! UNITED!' rang around

Old Trafford, with the home fans determined to show that they were up for this game. The away fans slipped in a shout of 'LEEDS' before each 'United', a tactic that turns the chant on its head with nothing the opposition can do about it, except to shut up.

On the journey to the game Paul said he would be happy if Leeds could just get a corner while it was 0-0, so that he could experience the surge of hope that would come with it (he presumed it would be the highlight of the match). He got his wish inside six minutes, and although we weren't stood together, it made me raise a smile for him. It was a good corner too, but Kuszczak's fists beat Becchio's head to the ball as the away fans let out an 'OOH' as if they'd just hit the post. Once ten minutes had passed Leeds were not only unscathed, they were giving as good as they got in a high-tempo, end-to-end battle. It must have given them such an adrenaline rush to be strutting their stuff in front of 75,000 at Old Trafford, when less than a week earlier they were playing in front of 7,500 down the road in Stockport.

A concerning little period followed, not helped by the referee, Chris Foy, who began to frustrate the Leeds fans with a series of soft calls in the home team's favour. One such decision, to penalise Kilkenny for obstructing Anderson, led to a free kick that was pumped into the Leeds half and plucked out of the air by Berbatov. The Bulgarian was instantly met by Richard Naylor, who muscled him off the ball, which broke to Jonny Howson near the far touchline. Howson's instinct was to look for Beckford, and a quick glance revealed half a pitch for Beckford to run into, if he could get his pass right. After two touches to set himself, Howson played a magnificent 50-yard ball over the top of Wes Brown and perfectly into the path of Beckford, who reached it on the edge of the box.

The Leeds fans held their breath as Beckford's control on his knee let him down, but with Kuszczak hesitant, Beckford reached the ball first and with a feather touch he prodded his shot through the lunging legs of the chasing defender, beyond the stretched leg of the onrushing goalkeeper and towards the far corner of the net. I've never seen a finish like it. It would have looked more at home on the 18th green at Augusta, and as it rolled towards the goal I was in disbelief, 'It's going in… it's actually going in… IT'S IN!' We went absolutely ballistic in the away end as Beckford wheeled away before being mobbed by his team-mates; what a moment for the former RAC windscreen fitter, a true FA Cup fairy tale.

Jermaine Beckford: 'As soon as Howson won the ball, with his technical ability and vision, I knew I just needed to get on Wes Brown's shoulder because in a foot race I was leaving him for dust! The delivery was inch perfect, right into my stride, but I got caught in two minds whether to control it on my right thigh or the inside of my left foot. The ball ran away from me but it turned into the best touch I could ever have imagined because it gave me three or four extra yards to get away from Wes Brown. I knew Brown would need to launch himself to make up the ground for a block, so I cut the ball underneath him, just beyond Kuszczak, and as I hit it the ball was heading outside the far post, and I'm thinking, "I think I've f*cked it!", but when you see it nestle into the far corner, it was magical. The commentator, Clive Tyldesley, said, "And it doesn't get any better than that for a Leeds United number nine," and he's not wrong. It was goosebumps then, and it's goosebumps now, it was incredible.'

If the goal galvanised anybody it was the visitors. The Leeds fans had barely finished celebrating when their team embarked upon their next attack with even more swagger than their first. It started with Johnson dancing round two players on the touchline in front of Sir Alex Ferguson, and a few slick passes later Kilkenny's cross from the opposite corner flag found Becchio eight yards out in the centre of the box. It should have been 2-0, but Becchio mis-timed his header and sent the ball high over the bar.

Old Trafford was clearly shocked at what it was witnessing, and what a moment it was to be a Leeds fan, but our joy should have lasted only five minutes as Berbatov's hooked volley sent Wayne Rooney sprinting through on goal. Rooney glanced up to see if there were any team-mates he could lay a sitter on for, but at that very moment Ankergren came rushing out and caught Rooney by surprise. The England striker hurriedly poked the ball towards goal, but Ankergren got enough of his body on the ball to delay its progress towards goal. It wasn't quite a save, but it was a vital intervention that enabled Crowe to sprint across and block the ball on the goal line, to the delighted cheers of the away fans. A minute later and it was Leeds's turn to rue another missed chance. Kilkenny was at the centre of it all again, and with four white shirts in the middle and only two red, Crowe picked out Johnson arriving at the far post but another poorly executed header looped harmlessly over the bar.

We were halfway through the first half and Leeds weren't only winning, they were the better team. I was in dreamland and I couldn't believe the levels we were reaching. Kilkenny was controlling the midfield, Kisnorbo and Naylor were going toe to toe with two world-class strikers, and the rest of the team were buzzing around, playing a vibrant brand of football like I hadn't seen since the O'Leary years. Aggressive and composed in equal measure, Grayson's team were peaking on the biggest stage.

Jonny Howson: 'Yeah, it does surprise you when you play like that against the calibre of players we were up against. For a lot of us, on paper this will have been the toughest game we'd had in our careers, but we held our own.'

For the next ten minutes the champions exerted their first period of sustained pressure, but this was repelled with relative comfort and the last ten minutes of the half turned scrappy. Mistakes were creeping into both teams' games and the rip-roaring opening 25 minutes took its toll on the tempo. When the half-time whistle blew the Leeds fans roared; they were halfway to their first Old Trafford victory in 29 years, a winless run that was older than me.

Simon Grayson: 'We started well and got the goal, but then you're worried we've scored too early and rattled their cages. We would have to keep working hard in the second half, keep our shape and discipline, but we had to make sure they knew they were in a game and the lads snapped into every tackle going.'

When the second half got under way Leeds continued as normal. Grayson's men clearly had no intention of holding on to what they had, nor were they daunted by the opposition, the venue, the occasion, or the position they found themselves in. Another sign of their mettle came when the first major flare-up happened on the edge of the Manchester United area. Brown flew into a nasty challenge on Doyle, Howson gained instant retribution, and a good old-fashioned melee ensued. In the end the referee gave a drop ball, and typical of the match it was Leeds who won it, with Becchio poking the ball towards the corner flag in front of us before Howson charged down Fábio's clearance for a goal kick. The Leeds fans celebrated vociferously. There's something magical about winning a drop ball, it's so raw, and once again the visitors had proved they wanted this more.

Jonny Howson: 'I always had the passion and determination to close people down, but I probably had a bit more fight in me because I'd grown up supporting Leeds United. Having the chance to go and play Man U away – our biggest rivals – there's no wonder you're going to give it everything. I'm no different to every fan that was in the ground or watching at home, I played it like one of them, giving it everything I've got and fighting for everything, and wanting to make the most of it.'

They may have wanted it more, but Manchester United had plenty in their locker to turn this around, and Ferguson soon introduced Ryan Giggs and Antonio Valencia, bringing a whole new challenge for Crowe and Hughes. They had dealt admirably with the young pretenders, now they faced two world-class wingers. Still, the home side struggled to stamp their authority on the match and suddenly we were into the last 25 minutes. Nearly three-quarters of the game had been played and League One Leeds were still beating the champions on their own patch.

On 70 minutes Ferguson had his last roll of the dice, bringing on Michael Owen for Anderson, and within a minute Valencia had laid a chance on a plate for the former Ballon d'Or winner, but Owen was caught cold and completely missed his kick with the goal gaping. Now just 19 minutes from glory, the Leeds fans were buoyant, 'NANA, NANA, NANA, NANA, NA, NA, NA. LEEDS ARE GOING UP, GOING UP, LEEDS ARE GOING UP!' The chant was flavour of the month and boomed from the away end to spur on the men in white.

On 77 minutes Robert Snodgrass replaced Jonny Howson, who received a well-deserved, resounding reception from the away fans.

What a performance the local lad had put in, and what a feeling it must have been to leave the Old Trafford pitch to the sound of 9,000 supporters singing your name.

Jonny Howson: 'I might have been a little disappointed to see my number come up, but that's just emotion. Once you've sat down you go into proper fan mode. I was just desperate for the lads to see the game out.'

Snodgrass's first act was to lose the ball timidly, but within seconds his determination had won it back, and a beautiful passage of one-touch passing bypassed the home midfield, then Doyle's pass to Beckford bypassed their defence. Beckford was in on goal again, and my heart skipped a beat as he took aim and fired from 16 yards, beyond the dive of Kuszczak but inches wide of the far post. What a goal it would have been. Was this the start of the hard-luck story?

The thought never entered the players' heads. Within two minutes they were attacking again and won a free kick 25 yards from goal, in the perfect position for Snodgrass. There was nobody else in contention, only Snodgrass stood over the ball, and with hands clasped together I prayed for Snoddy to come up with something special. He did exactly that, whipping in a stunning effort that cannoned off the angle of post and bar, shaking the frame of the goal with the goalkeeper well and truly beaten. There was no time to wonder 'what if?' as within seconds the home side were on the counter-attack. Berbatov fed Owen, who fell in the box under pressure from Andy Hughes. Old Trafford screamed for a penalty, their players frantically waved their arms and my heart was in my mouth, but the referee waved play on. Thank goodness. There would be nothing worse than a disputable penalty bailing out Ferguson's men.

We were into the last ten minutes. As time ticked on the inevitability of an equaliser was diminishing, and the home fans were starting to sense disaster – maybe the impossible was possible? An injury to Becchio ran down a couple more minutes, and by the time he'd left the pitch there were just two minutes to go. After tackling the champions of England face-on for 88 minutes, Grayson finally wound his neck in and replaced his striker with a defender, big Ľubomír Michalík, a sensible move with the fourth official about to indicate five minutes of added time.

Simon Grayson: 'When injury time goes up my first thoughts were, "Fergie Time", they're gonna score at least one and take us to a replay, or maybe even two!'

Now that we were so tantalisingly close, survival was the only target for Leeds, and they survived their biggest scare when Valencia's cross deflected into the path of Rooney, arriving on the penalty spot to smash a volley towards goal. Ankergren was equal to it, parrying the ball against Fábio then reacting quickest to deny Owen a tap-in. But the ball bounced back into the middle of the goalmouth, where 11 players were waiting to pounce in and around the six-yard box. The ball fell to Doyle, who showed a composure that could only be expected from the greatest players ever to have graced a football pitch, skipping around Gibson before reverting to type and hacking into touch with his weaker right foot. There were gasps from the away end, but the lead was still intact.

The Whites were still under siege, but when Rooney's wild slice sent the ball into the Stretford End the Leeds fans finally started to believe, and burst into giddy celebrations. Surely that was it, surely this goal kick would bring the curtain down on this epic FA Cup classic? The whistles were ringing out from the away end but still the ref didnt blow, and when he did it wasn't for full time, though it was still greeted by an enormous cheer from the travelling fans as they had won a free kick on the halfway line. 'PUT IT IN THE FUCKING CORNER LEEDS!' This was not a scream of fear or desperation, it was excited jubilation for what was about to happen. I now believed we were going to pull off the impossible win, time was up, no question, this was actually it!

The Leeds fans around me were bouncing up and down singing 'Leeds are going up' while those in the top tier behind the goal sang about going to Wembley, and the rest of Old Trafford was sat in stunned silence. They hadn't experienced such a result in over 20 years, Alex Ferguson had never lost to a lower-league side in the FA Cup, and nor had he ever lost in the third round. Grayson's team were seconds away from changing all of that.

Johnson sent the free kick towards the corner flag, and as Beckford shepherded the ball Foy blew the full-time whistle and the away end erupted as if they had just seen a last-minute winner. Leeds had done it! They had beaten their arch-rivals, the champions of England and back-to-back Champions League finalists, at Old Trafford, in the FA Cup, as a League One team! I couldn't fucking believe it! All I had ever known in football was what ifs and heartbreak – Italia '90, the 1994 World Cup, Euro '96, the O'Leary years, relegations, play-off final defeats – and finally, finally, the football gods had given me my miracle moment, the best match of my life!

Casper Ankergren: 'To win at Old Trafford was one of the highlights of my career without a doubt. To see how much it meant to the fans was something very special. I'll remember it for the rest of my life.'

Jermaine Beckford's name was the first to ring out from the euphoric away end, but despite being the match-winner it seemed inappropriate. To a man, every Leeds player had played the game of their lives. 'One Simon Grayson' soon took over, and that felt more fitting; what a job he had done, what an achievement to overcome Sir Alex Ferguson. He had given his fellow Leeds fans their best moment since winning the league title in 1992. The emotions barely subsided during a long lock-in while the home fans went home. Eventually we were let out and I said goodbye to the young boy I had shared the happiest day of my life with.

> *Simon Grayson: 'They had a real good team out, and some top players on the bench too, but we were value for money. Casper made a couple of good saves and we made some blocks, and they missed a couple of chances, but we were in those positions as well and looked like we could score again. We defended as a team, individuals put their hearts and souls into it, and when the final whistle goes you're just thinking, "Wow. We've done it!"'*

We got home and went straight to The Alex to continue the celebrations, meeting up with Rick and Terry who were still partying themselves. We arrived in time for the fourth round draw and it was another classic, with Leeds the last team out of the hat for the second round running. Once Chelsea were drawn there was only one tie we wanted, and each ball drew a buoyant cheer as we were handed a trip to White Hart Lane to face Harry Redknapp's high-flying Tottenham. It was another fantastic draw, the tie of the round again, and another chance for Leeds to show what they might be capable of, if they were able to achieve back-to-back promotions with this fantastic squad Simon Grayson had assembled.

> *Bradley Johnson: As players, we didn't really get to celebrate it as we had another game coming up. It wasn't until I watched the game back with Snoddy and Becks in lockdown [in 2020] that I realised how well we had played and just what an achievement it was.'*

> *Luciano Becchio: 'We were what Leeds are historically.'*

195

Tottenham Hotspur 2 Leeds United 2

FA Cup fourth round
White Hart Lane (35,750)

> *'To go and put in another top performance against another*
> *of the top sides in the country, away from home, you start*
> *to realise we've got some very good players here.' – Jonny*
> *Howson*

Football is a funny old game. Within a week of beating
Manchester United news had broken that match-winner
Jermaine Beckford was back on the transfer list, and Leeds had
struggled to a 1-1 draw against Wycombe Wanderers, League
One's second-bottom team. Grayson admitted it was a case of
'after the Lord Mayor's Show' but his side still remained six
points clear at the top of the table.

The following week the gap was cut to three points after
United fell to an insipid 2-0 defeat at lowly Exeter City.
Millwall and Liverpool had been the only other teams to beat
Grayson's side through the season, but four days later Carlisle
added themselves to the list with a 2-1 victory at Elland Road
in the northern area final (aka the semi-final) of the Football
League Trophy. It was an alarming run of results, but the FA
Cup provided an escape from the humdrum life as a lower-
league club and it was time to mix it with the best again.

By the time Leeds took to the pitch at White Hart Lane,
Norwich had overtaken them at the top of League One, but
at least Beckford's immediate future was no longer in doubt.
After Newcastle refused to increase their bid beyond £1.5m
Bates drew a line in the sand, deciding once and for all that
Beckford would see out the season at Elland Road. The
decision had the blessing of the player too, who was quoted
on the club's official website as saying, 'I want to finish what
I've been striving to do for the last two seasons. I want to help

promote Leeds out of a division they don't belong in. Every time I put on the Leeds United shirt I give 100 per cent, and can assure the fans, manager, and everyone connected with the club that I will continue to do that.' It was time for Beckford to get back to the business of scoring goals.

Leeds's task at Tottenham was arguably harder than the one they faced at Old Trafford. Redknapp had done a terrific job since replacing Juande Ramos just over a year earlier, taking Spurs from the bottom of the Premier League to challenging for a Champions League qualification place. Now Spurs were fourth, and fielding practically a full-strength team: Brazil's Heurelho Gomes in goal, Scotland's Alan Hutton at right-back, Wales's Gareth Bale at left-back, Cameroon's Sébastien Bassong alongside Northallerton's Michael Dawson at centre-back, an England–Croatia tag-team in midfield with Luca Modrić and Jermaine Jenas in the middle and Niko Kranjčar and Danny Rose out wide, and England strikers Peter Crouch and Jermain Defoe up front. A daunting prospect for United was exacerbated by the absence of Richard Naylor and Luciano Becchio. Leigh Bromby would deputise for the inspirational captain and Robert Snodgrass got the nod to partner Beckford in attack, otherwise, it was 'as you were' from Old Trafford.

Jermaine Beckford: 'I grew up as an Arsenal fan and still have a soft spot for them, so playing their north London rivals, at an amazing stadium like White Hart Lane against a team with so many incredible footballers, it gave it an extra edge. Before the game Jermain Defoe told me he loved what we did to Man United, and to hear that from a player I was in awe of really spurred me on.'

This match fell on Paul's birthday weekend and we planned a trip to London to celebrate with his brother Nige and whoever else was up for it, either side of going to the game.

Unfortunately for the birthday boy we failed to get tickets but, fortunately for me, Lewis managed to conjure one up and I was spared the disappointment of missing what was sure to be a great occasion, no matter the result. I broke away from the birthday celebrations in Angel and headed to White Hart Lane on the tube, with plenty of time to spare in case I messed up the journey. It wasn't hard to get right, but I was scuppered by line closures which tested my competence and patience to the limit. Worse still, Lewis had come down on the coach and had possession of my ticket, so when it became clear that I was going to miss kick-off I was even more stressed about forcing him to miss the opening too, or even worse, that he would sack me off and go in without me!

I finally arrived at Seven Sisters and with a mobile phone signal I could finally alert Lewis of my whereabouts. I was relieved to hear that Lewis had suffered the same predicament as me, but not so pleased that he caused me to be even later. We were so late into the ground that I only found out Ankergren had saved a 20th-minute Defoe penalty when watching the highlights the following day. The visitors' allocation stretched from the corner to the middle of the goal, which helped to build an electric atmosphere, as did the Saturday evening kick-off time and the fact that the clubs hadn't faced each other for almost a decade. They may or may not admit it, but other clubs love welcoming Leeds to their ground. The away end is guaranteed to be packed out and relentlessly vocal, bringing the best out of the home fans, and White Hart Lane was super-charged. It hit me as soon as I entered the ground.

The first action I saw was a Kranjčar free kick spilled by Ankergren, but fortunately Kisnorbo was alert and got his body in the way of Defoe's follow-up. Immediately Leeds glided upfield with the same poise and purpose we had seen at Old Trafford, but rarely since. It came to nothing but it really got my juices flowing. Were we in for another FA Cup classic?

Kilkenny was dictating the play, Doyle a tiger alongside him, and Beckford's pace was a constant threat in behind. Snodgrass gave Leeds a new dimension though. The young Scotsman was thriving in a central role and drew a good save from Gomes with a curling effort from the edge of the box, then laid a chance into the path of Beckford who forced another good stop from the goalkeeper. Faced with a stronger, more cohesive team than in round three, Leeds were still giving as good as they got.

'ARE YOU WATCHING, ARE YOU WATCHING, ARE YOU WATCHING, MANCHESTER?' asked the Leeds fans, eager to milk their fleeting superiority over their cross-Pennine rivals, but in the closing stages of the half Spurs broke the deadlock when Crouch converted after Ankergren saved from Kranjčar. It was a lead the hosts probably deserved, and Jenas should have doubled that lead but blasted a clear chance over the bar seconds before half-time. Seconds after the break Beckford should have wiped the lead out when he pounced on a loose back-pass, but his touch around the keeper was too heavy and the ball rolled out of play. In case they needed reminding, Spurs were still in a cup tie. Five minutes later, it was 1-1.

Jermaine Beckford: 'Snoddy swung a corner in and the ball dropped to me in the six-yard box. I swivelled and got a toe poke on it as I fell to the ground, and when the ball rolled into the net the eruption of the Leeds fans behind the goal was incredible. I should have been used to it by then, but it still gave me goosebumps. Some of my best mates are Spurs fans and they'd been mouthing off before the game, so scoring against them made it even sweeter!'

Now the League One side had the bit between their teeth, and the yellow shirts piled forward looking to capitalise on their moment of superiority. Just after the hour Snodgrass tormented Tottenham again, driving forward, evading challenges before playing a lovely one-two with Kilkenny. The Australian's cute back-heel wasn't quite perfect though, and on the stretch Snodgrass couldn't control his finish with the ball going harmlessly wide. The Leeds players were brimming with confidence and the away fans were cheering their every pass. I wondered what the Spurs fans must have thought as their third-tier opponents knocked the ball around with such assurance. Who could expect a team from that level to play like this?

On 70 minutes Redknapp called for the cavalry. On came Robbie Keane and Roman Pavlyuchenko – another £30m of striking talent for Kisnorbo and Bromby, £250,000 of centre-backs, to deal with – and £12m Wilson Palacios was added to the midfield. Five minutes later, a great interchange between Palacios, Bale, Defoe and Pavlyuchenko cut the Leeds defence open and the Russian striker finished with aplomb. It was a goal that oozed Premier League quality.

Grayson responded by calling for his own cavalry, bringing on Becchio. Leeds's front three of Beckford, Snodgrass and Becchio cost £450,000, while Spurs' trio of Defoe, Pavlyuchenko and Keane cost £45m, but Goliath couldn't deliver the killer blow. Spurs had a goal disallowed and another effort hooked off the line but while there was one goal in the game there was still hope, and David was clinging on to the ropes. The announcement of a generous five minutes of injury time signalled a change in momentum, and for the majority of it Leeds pegged Tottenham back deep in their own half. Now it was Goliath who was clinging on to the ropes.

In the 94th minute, with all hope almost gone, Beckford received the ball in the box but couldn't get away from Dawson, who made a superb sliding tackle. Beckford appealed and the

Leeds fans screamed for a penalty, but it was purely out of desperation. There were now just 30 seconds remaining and Bale was steaming forward on the counter-attack, until he was stopped in his tracks by Jason Crowe and the ball found Howson in space. Howson's instinct, as always, was to look for Beckford.

Jonny Howson: 'I played a lot of reserve-team football up front with Jermaine, so we had a good understanding and I knew that the majority of the time he wanted the ball in behind because of his pace, and it worked to great effect many times for Leeds.'

After a quick glance, Howson launched another raking 50-yard ball to the edge of the box, not dissimilar to the pass of his career at Old Trafford. This time Beckford's touch was perfect, enabling him to face up Dawson and run at him one last time.

Jermaine Beckford: 'I wanted to lure Dawson in and take it on my right and shoot, but once I was in the box I gave him the shimmy and took him on the outside. He lunged in and got me just before he got the ball, and fortunately the referee saw it exactly as it was and gave the penalty. I was over the moon but then came the hard bit, and waiting to take the penalty seemed to go on for an age. When you're playing for a humongous club like Leeds, apart from the thousands in the stadium there's millions of fans around the world that are glued to that exact moment, and if you mess it up you're going to know about it! So to have the ability to blank all that stuff out and have a clear mindset of what to do in that moment is tough.'

With the clock ticking around to 96 minutes, the referee blew his whistle and all eyes were on Beckford. Pessimistic old me fully expected him to bottle it, but the former Wealdstone striker was ice-cool, side-footing firmly into the top corner, and when the net bulged the away end burst into jubilant celebrations again. 'They are quite something! What a travelling army! What a team! What an FA Cup story!' The commentator on ITV was almost as excited as me, but I was over-excited, to such an extent that when I realised I'd lost my phone in all the commotion I didn't even care. The battery from my Samsung Galaxy was on the floor by my feet, but a quick scan brought no sign of the gadget itself. That was insignificant compared to the match though, which was about to restart with Leeds only moments away from a money-spinning replay. Seconds later the away fans were cheering the final whistle, and they and their team would do it all again at Elland Road in ten days' time.

Casper Ankergren: 'Our performances in those cup ties showed that we had Premier League players, they just weren't Premier League players yet.'

After saluting our heroes, the panic set in. Without my phone there would be no way of meeting up with my mates and I would be completely stranded in London. We were locked in the ground which bought me more time to try and locate it, and after a couple of minutes of searching one of my lovely comrades patted me on the shoulder and handed me the phone they had found. Phew!

Before we left the players came out for a quick warm-down, enabling us to pay homage one more time. They were all heroes, and not only could I not wait to see them take on the elite with 40,000 backing them under the lights at Elland Road, I couldn't wait for the draw for the last 16. I was dreaming of Wembley.

Leeds United 1 Tottenham Hotspur 3

FA Cup fourth round replay
Elland Road (37,704)

> *'Night games at Elland Road, with the top tier open and a*
> *full house, you can't beat them.' – Bradley Johnson*

With Arsenal, Liverpool and Manchester United already out, there really weren't many teams left to fear. You could legitimately argue that League One Leeds were, historically, the biggest club left in the draw, and Chelsea were the only elite side, while Manchester City were two seasons into their new status as the richest club in the world and would present very difficult opposition. Otherwise, the remaining clubs were Football League sides or Premier League strugglers, and Leeds drew one of the latter, Bolton Wanderers away. I truly felt that if we could beat Spurs at Elland Road we would go to the Reebok, where we were relegated six years earlier, and gain our revenge. Then with a decent quarter-final draw, who knows what could happen?

Two days after the Spurs game came more good news for Leeds. Max Gradel had handed in a transfer request at Leicester, paving the way for a permanent move to Elland Road which was duly completed for an undisclosed fee. What a fantastic transfer window this was turning into. Leeds had signed a brilliant young winger, retained one of the hottest strikers in the country, and had also retained their manager, with Simon Grayson rebuffing the advances of Premier League Burnley. Surely no other League One manager had ever, or would have, turned down a job in the big league.

Simon Grayson: 'I was approached to be Burnley manager.
Of course I wanted to manage in the Premier League, but I

wanted to fulfil that ambition with my club and that's why I didn't accept it.'

The following weekend it was back to the grindstone of League One football. Grayson's men got the job done this time with a 2-0 victory over Colchester courtesy of another Beckford brace, but the absence of Kilkenny and Kisnorbo raised concerns ahead of the Tottenham replay and afterwards Grayson confirmed that neither would be available. It was a body blow to Leeds's chances to lose two players who had been a cornerstone of their sensational form.

Jermaine Beckford: 'Losing Kisnorbo was a huge blow, and I loved playing with Kilkenny. He had a great knack of finding five yards of space, and always had a picture of what he was going to do before he actually did it. We missed him when he wasn't in the team, for that yappy mouth of his if nothing else!'

At least Leeds would have almost 40,000 vociferous fans on their side, and the Yorkshire weather. In freezing conditions, with snow shovelled to the sides of a struggling pitch, Elland Road was absolutely rocking when the teams emerged from the tunnel; the atmosphere was as fervent as any European night. However, Tottenham's all-star team took it in their stride, and just two minutes into the game Defoe was sent through. His scuffed finish beat Ankergren but might not have reached the goal even if Richard Naylor wasn't on hand to clear to safety. Nevertheless, it was a worrying start.

Defoe had three more chances in the next 30 minutes; twice he was denied by Ankergren, and once he drilled wide of the far post. Leeds were huffing and puffing but the gulf in class seemed to be catching up with them. After 37 minutes Spurs did take the lead, and it was fifth time lucky for Defoe, really lucky. He swiped at a bouncing ball in the box, shinning it high into the air to the delight of the Kop, who cheered ironically until it looped down into the top corner of the net. It was a cruel way to break Leeds's resistance but it sparked them into life. The rest of the half was played in Tottenham territory and with Snodgrass the main source of threat, Bale just couldn't get to grips with his quick feet and trickery. In stoppage time Snodgrass's corner was only cleared as far as Howson, who hooked it back into the box where Beckford was unmarked and onside. Beckford's instinctive volley was saved by Gomes, but Becchio was on hand to turn in the rebound and send Elland Road delirious. The Wembley dream was alive and kicking.

The second half continued at a rip-roaring pace. The fans were giving as much as the players, but without Kilkenny in midfield Leeds struggled to hold any sustained periods of possession. Counter-attacks and the odd set piece were all the home side could muster, otherwise it was all Spurs. Ankergren was proving to be a stubborn last line of defence and when Spurs finally got the ball in the net with 22 minutes remaining it was the linesman's turn to deny Defoe. However, there was no denying the little striker five minutes later when he turned in David Bentley's low cross from close range. The Wembley dream was slipping away, but you wouldn't have known it as Elland Road burst into a deafening version of 'Marching On Together' to stimulate United for one last big push.

Despite the Kop's best efforts, Leeds just couldn't summon the quality to force another equaliser. An 89th-minute free kick was headed wide by Michalík, and in the 94th minute, with everyone up for one last pump into the box, Spurs' last-ditch clearance sent Defoe clean through to seal the victory and his hat-trick. There could be no denying who had deserved to win, but Redknapp still lavished praise on the home side and their fans, 'We came to Elland Road, probably for the first time for some of my players, and the atmosphere the fans created was just incredible.' Leeds's valiant FA Cup adventure was over, but the Wembley dream hadn't ended just yet.

A week later Leeds headed to Carlisle for the second leg of the Football League Trophy northern area final, with a place at Wembley up for grabs. Having dropped two more points at the weekend, thanks to a 93rd-minute Hartlepool United equaliser at Victoria Park, Grayson's men really needed the pick-me-up of reaching a final, even if it would arguably be a stain on the club's history to win the Football League Trophy. I had never attended a Football League Trophy game for that very reason, but now that we had come so far I really didn't want all our cup exploits to have been in vain, and this team deserved to do the League One and Football League Trophy double.

In a replica of the 2008 play-offs, Leeds's task was to overcome a 2-1 deficit away to Carlisle, but at half-time that had become a 3-1 aggregate deficit and with ten minutes to go it was 4-2, trailing 2-1 on the night. Yet the weary Whites rallied with goals from Jason Crowe and Mike Grella to force extra time and then penalties, but an epic shoot-out was eventually won by the home side. Carlisle would face Southampton at Wembley and their fans were ecstatic, invading the pitch and attacking some of the Leeds players in their over-zealous celebrations. What a night. It was the last thing Grayson needed, and probably a bigger blow to him and his squad than to the supporters, who at least would save some hard-earned brass.

Simon Grayson: 'You don't get many opportunities to play at Wembley, and even in the JPT [Johnstone's Paint Trophy, as the competition was known at the time for sponsorship purposes] Leeds would have taken their full allocation, so it would have been an unbelievable atmosphere. And from a personal point of view, leading Leeds United out at Wembley would have been an incredible feeling. So to lose on penalties was a big disappointment.'

———

Leeds United 1 Walsall 2

Matchday 30 of 46
Elland Road (18,941)

'We'd played a lot of games, and going from the highs of the FA Cup and back to League One, it's tricky to juggle. You see it with teams playing in Europe still today, it's always happened.' – Casper Ankergren

Finally, after seven epic cup ties in eight weeks (well six, as you can't count the Carlisle home leg as epic), it was time to concentrate on the league, but Leeds slipped up again, needing a 95th-minute own goal to salvage a point from their trip to Leyton Orient. It was now one win in six league matches and Norwich had built a four-point lead at the top, although Leeds still had two games in hand. More importantly, Leeds were still five points clear of third-placed Charlton, with a game more to play too. With such a comfortable gap inside the automatic promotion places there was no need to panic, especially with a full week to recharge the batteries ahead of three home games in seven days, against mid-table Walsall, and relegation-battling Brighton and Oldham. Nine points would put Leeds back in control of the title race, and promotion would once again look a formality.

Not that anybody at Elland Road was taking promotion for granted. Ken Bates sanctioned a busy January transfer window, following up the signing of Max Gradel with the addition of Shane Lowry on loan from Aston Villa. Grayson had high hopes that Lowry would rectify a problem at left-back which had persisted all season, with Ben Parker,

Aidy White and Tony Capaldi failing there due to injury, inexperience, and ineptitude respectively. Andy Hughes had done an admirable job as a makeshift solution, but a specialist left-back was a clear way to improve the team and would allow Hughes to take up a more natural (but still not completely natural) role at right-back, where neither Crowe nor Bromby had truly convinced.

There was still room for one more loan signing, which really got my pulse racing. Birmingham City winger Gary McSheffrey had cost them £4m, and was their top scorer when they won promotion to the Premier League in 2007. Three years later his career had stalled, but I was still shocked that a player of his quality would drop down to League One. Surely he would tear this division up. With Snodgrass, Gradel, Johnson and Robinson already vying for the wing positions, Grayson was certainly adding from a position of strength.

To make way for the new additions some fringe players were cast aside, including cult hero David Prutton. 'Jesus' moved to Colchester for first-team football and left with a heavy heart, sending an open letter to the Leeds fans which he signed off beautifully, 'Leeds fans are loud, loyal and passionate. Make no mistake, you are the lifeblood of the club and always will be. You were always fantastic to me and I hold that in my heart as I move on. Thanks for everything.'

David Prutton: 'The final nail in the coffin for me came after I cut my hair. I wasn't in the team and the Elland Road MC wanted to get me on the pitch at half-time. I know I'm game for a laugh but there's no way I'm going out at Elland Road just because I've had my hair cut! If that was my stature at the club it was probably best to look elsewhere! I was genuinely gutted to leave, but I'll always be an ex-Leeds United player and nobody can ever take that away from me.'

It was sad to see Prutton go, but Leeds looked stronger than ever heading into the last 17 games. The cups were history, it was time to go hell for leather for the League One title.

Under Grayson, Elland Road was a bona fide fortress. Since a defeat in his second home game Leeds had gone 13 months and 26 league games unbeaten, and nobody saw that run ending any time soon, not least on a Tuesday night against Walsall. After a lacklustre first half the Whites fell behind a minute into the second when a stunning volley from the edge of the box flew into Ankergren's bottom corner, but when McSheffrey's poor cross somehow floated past the keeper and into the net everybody expected an onslaught and the winning goal. Far from it. Walsall deservedly grabbed a scrappy winner from a late corner, even if Ankergren appeared to have clawed the ball off the goal line. The final whistle brought boos from the Elland Road faithful, and Grayson fumed in his post-match interview, 'We got out of the game exactly what we deserved, nothing. We just had nothing about us, none of the players did themselves any justice.'

> Jonny Howson: 'The emotion of the cup games, and that bit of success on the big stage, it did take something away from us in the league. The mental side of it is tough, you've just beat Man U away and next you've got Wycombe at home. You haven't got that natural buzz, that excitement.'

After the game I was panicking. How could a team that had steamrolled the division, and played so well against the best teams in the country, suddenly be playing so terribly? How long would it take for us to rediscover our confidence? Could we handle the pressure? The questions stirring around my head found their way out of my mouth when my mate Adam called me as I drove the van home from the game. Adam and I aired all our concerns and it was a big help. We concluded that we were surely panicking prematurely. Yes, McSheffrey was poor, but he was still rusty and getting up to match fitness. Yes, Beckford was struggling, but he'd still score goals. Yes, Grayson was chopping and changing, but there was plenty in that squad to get us out of the league comfortably. Yes, we'd feel much better after dispatching Brighton and Oldham.

Grayson was also sure his team would be back to their normal selves for the weekend visit of Brighton, but they weren't. With Gradel, Becchio and Snodgrass all left on the bench, Leeds were toothless and appeared to be heading for another defeat when Glenn Murray converted a 77th-minute penalty for Gus Poyet's third-bottom team. The ineffective McSheffrey was immediately withdrawn, then Brighton were reduced to ten men, and United huffed and puffed, and in the 95th minute Snodgrass popped up with a scrappy equaliser. But there was no Elland Road Shuffle in the Kop; a point was measly and we needed all three. Grayson didn't agree, insisting it could be a vital draw come the end of the season.

Three days later Leeds did get back to winning ways, beating Oldham 2-0 thanks to Becchio's quickfire brace at the beginning of the second half. It was a much-improved performance and the victory opened up a four-point gap over Prutton's third-placed Colchester. Norwich had won again, but Leeds, who still had a game in hand, were within striking distance of top spot heading into the West Yorkshire derby.

———

Huddersfield Town 2 Leeds United 2

Matchday 33 of 46
Galpharm Stadium (21,764)

'Every away game was a cup final for the opposition. I'd go to scout an opponent and the ground would be half empty, with nobody bothered about singing a song. But when we

turned up it would be a full house, the fans had found their voice, and players were raising their games by at least 50 per cent.' – Simon Grayson

The short trip to Huddersfield was made slightly shorter as it coincided with my first trip to Manchester (when I wasn't just visiting a stadium). It was Adam's stag do, and after a very messy Friday night it wasn't easy to force myself out of bed and over to Huddersfield for a lunchtime kick-off, but by the time I'd taken my place in the away end I was bang up for it. So too were the home side and they dominated a feisty first half, peppering the goal in front of us and taking the lead when one of their efforts wickedly deflected past Ankergren.

At half-time it was a relief Leeds were still in the game, and in the second half they came out looking a rejuvenated team. As the clock ticked past the hour, Jonny Howson picked up the ball in midfield, rode two challenges and fed Snodgrass on the right. A 'Cruyff turn' left his marker for dead, and Snoddy's cross found the head of Howson, who had continued his run into the box and sent a perfect glancing header into the bottom corner of the net. The Leeds-born youngster celebrated passionately in front of the away end – the perfect goal at the perfect time, by the perfect player.

Jonny Howson: 'It definitely meant more, being at Huddersfield. In League One it was our biggest game, and they had a decent side that was going for the play-offs. I've still got that photo of me running off in front of the away fans and kissing the badge.'

Leeds's tails were firmly up now, and they completed the turnaround when a Snodgrass corner was flicked on at the near post then touched into the net by Becchio, causing pandemonium in the away end. It had turned into a fantastic, end-to-end match. Lee Clarke's Terriers were desperate to extend a ten-game unbeaten run that had catapulted them into the play-off places, while Leeds were desperate to claim much-needed consecutive victories, and a first win at Huddersfield's 16-year-old stadium. Sadly it was Clarke who got his wish, his side conjuring up the equaliser with five minutes left. In the end a draw was a fair result, although Grayson admitted he would be the happier of the two managers despite conceding a late equaliser. I was happy enough too. Leeds had played like their pre-Old Trafford selves in the second half and showed plenty of heart against a good side in a partisan atmosphere. Surely now we could push on to promotion.

Not quite. The following Saturday, mid-table Brentford came to Elland Road and again Leeds stuttered to a 1-1 home draw, falling behind for the fifth time in six matches but rescuing another point thanks to Beckford's first goal in nine games. With the last attack of the match a shooting chance was presented to Michael Doyle on the edge of the box, and when his 20-yard effort flew hopelessly into the Kop the frustration of the past two months overcame me. I launched into a furious tirade of abuse at Doyle, which resulted in me almost fainting. I had to grab the seat next to me to keep my balance, and remained seated for the final seconds. It was a sign of the stress everyone at the club was now under, as promotion seemed to be slipping away. Charlton were just two points behind Leeds, while Norwich were a massive seven points clear. Leeds still had a game in hand, but what good are games in hand when you can't win?

Jonny Howson: 'We'd failed in the past two seasons, which added to the pressure when we started going through a rocky patch. You can't not look at the table, you turn the TV on and it pops up, and I was just thinking, "We can't go into the play-offs," 'cos we're not very good at the play-offs!'

It had been two months since the Old Trafford victory, and after every night out I'd re-watched the match when getting home (though I'd often fall asleep before we'd even taken the lead). However, with our season in dire straits I could no longer bear to watch, I was petrified that the victory would be soured forever by costing us promotion. After the draw with Brentford my last action before bed was to update my Facebook status with a simple prayer, 'Dear Lord, please let Leeds get promoted this season. Amen.'

The game in hand was at struggling Tranmere three days later, coinciding with a first vs second battle in the Nidderdale Snooker League. Thankfully there was little distraction from Prenton Park – by the time I took the table it was half-time and Leeds had raced into a 3-1 lead, on their way to a confidence-boosting 4-1 thrashing. It wasn't the only thrashing of the night as Birstwith lost 5-1 to Pateley, effectively sealing our fate as runners-up again, but as one title race ended another was back on. It's amazing how one result can completely change your mindset; a run of just two wins in 11 had suddenly become a run of just three defeats in 22. Everything was going to be OK.

Southampton 1 Leeds United 0

Matchday 36 of 46
St Mary's Stadium (30,794)

> 'You have to be mentally strong to be a footballer, but you
> have to be twice as mentally strong as other players when
> you're playing for Leeds United, because of the expectancy
> level that comes with the honour of playing for them.' –
> Simon Grayson

After Tranmere came the long trip to Southampton, who boasted the most expensive squad in League One history but were still 16 points off the play-off places. Paul and I made the journey down to St Mary's, which turned into a thoroughly miserable day out. The Saints played Leeds off the park in front of a buoyant home crowd, and the drive home felt even longer due to who the match-winner was.

Of all the players in the Southampton team – Rickie Lambert, Adam Lallana, Morgan Schneiderlin, Jason Puncheon, and with Alex Oxlade-Chamberlain on the bench – it was former Leeds left-back Dan Harding who scored the only goal of the game. The Leeds fans had been subjected to a long list of inadequate left-backs since Tony Dorigo was named their Player of the Year in 1993: Nigel Worthington, David Robertson, Danny Granville, Raúl Bravo and Stephen Crainey had been afflicted with Elland Road's left-back curse, which even eventually got to Ian Harte, who had been one of the most dangerous full-backs in Europe but was now also playing in League One, for Carlisle. Harding added his name to the list with 20 weak performances following a £450,000 move from Brighton, but now back in the safe haven of the south coast he was a strong and confident full-back, and midway through the half he found himself in the penalty area and hit the back of the net. Harding celebrated by running along the away end and berating the travelling fans who had berated him for a season. What goes around comes around I suppose.

As we set off on the long drive home my mood was further darkened by the news that Norwich had won again, stretching their lead at the top to seven points. The title that had looked in the bag only a few weeks earlier now seemed to be destined for Carrow Road. However, finishing in the top two was all that really mattered, and Charlton had been thrashed 4-0 by Millwall which kept the gap to third at five points, with ten games remaining. There was more relief when I was stopped by the police as we arrived back in Harrogate. My eagerness to end the god-forsaken trip caused me to drive over the speed limit, but fortunately the policeman's speed gun had failed to discharge and there was no evidence with which to charge me. A ticking-off was politely taken and I was even afforded some sympathy when explaining my football-related plight.

Leeds's next game was against Millwall, televised live on *Monday Night Football*. There was no Beckford as he was ruled out with a hamstring strain and in his place came Paul Dickov, who had signed a short-term contract until the end of the season. A passionate and experienced striker, he wouldn't carry the threat of Beckford but he was sure to give his all for the cause, and if his impact was anything like that of Dougie Freedman's then Leeds would be just fine.

With Norwich and Charlton both held to draws at the weekend, Leeds knew that three points would have them chasing top spot again rather than looking over their shoulder. However, a season that had turned on its head took a massive nosedive in the 12th minute when Paddy Kisnorbo collapsed in a heap during the build-up to Steve Morison opening the scoring for Millwall. The sight of Kisnorbo being stretchered off was as painful as the goal, and worse news would follow as the Australian had ruptured his Achilles. Our star defender's season was over, as was his dream of playing in the 2010 World Cup. Leeds were unable to respond to the seismic double blow and produced another feeble performance, registering only one shot on target and only two corners over the 90 minutes. Millwall secured a 2-0 win when their winger Shaun Batt danced past two challenges with criminal ease and beat Ankergren at his near post. It was a goal that summed up Leeds's display; their confidence was in pieces.

The promotion race had been blown wide open, and with ten wins in their last 12 games, Millwall had cut what was a 21-point gap at the turn of the year down to three. I was starting to wonder how the players could turn things around.

Bradley Johnson: 'It was a difficult time. I'd been at the club three seasons and every year the expectation was to get out of the league, and rightly so. We'd failed twice, and now we were going through another dip. The fans were getting itchy and it was difficult to play at Elland Road for three or four games, the pressure got to us, I think you could see that in our performances. But the experienced players in the dressing room were massive for us – Casper, Naylor, Hughesy – and Simon just maintained that we were a good team and everyone goes through bad patches, we just needed to keep on doing what we were doing and believe in ourselves.'

It never rains but it pours, and next up was a trip to table-topping Norwich, who had won ten of their last 13. Grayson recalled Shane Higgs in goal, reinstated Neil Kilkenny in midfield, and replaced Kisnorbo with an emergency loan signing. Neil Collins was a no-nonsense centre-back who had won promotions to the Premier League with both Sunderland and Wolverhampton Wanderers, without being a regular in either side and without a top-flight appearance to his name. Although he lacked the class of Kisnorbo, Grayson must have been pleased to get a centre-back of his experience at this stage of the season.

The reshuffled team put in a solid display at Carrow Road, but in the 89th minute Chris Martin beat Collins to a near-post cross and condemned Leeds to a third straight defeat. The title race was over – Norwich were 11 points clear, surely home and hosed – but much worse for Leeds was the disappearance of the gap to third. Millwall's 5-0 victory over Stockport had drawn them level on points with the Whites, only behind on goal difference, by one goal. The situation was dire.

I wasn't at Norwich; instead me and my mates had gone for a night out in Leeds, although it was more of a full-day event, and almost a two-day event in the end. We drank and played pool in Walkabout sports bar while Leeds fell to defeat, after which I was ready to drink myself into a stupor to forget my football woes. It didn't work. My mates dragged me to Basics, a club they loved but wasn't really my thing, although I stayed and for a while I enjoyed myself. At 5am it was time for the 'after-party', but by now I was back to worrying about Leeds, ignoring the fairer sex and spending all my time chatting up lads, with the opening line, 'Are you a Leeds fan, mate?' I just needed someone to talk to.

I was so worried, not only about promotion, but about Simon Grayson's future. I felt sure Ken Bates was going to lose his nerve and sack our beloved manager. We finally left and headed to the train station with the morning sun on the rise, and as I walked through the city centre I chanted on repeat, at the very top of my voice, emphasising every syllable, 'ONE SIMON GRAYSON! THERE'S ONLY ONE SIMON GRAYSON! ONE SIMON GRAAAAAAYSON! THERE'S ONLY ONE SIMON GRAYSON!'

—

Leeds United 0 Swindon Town 3

Matchday 39 of 46
Elland Road (27,881)

> *'I felt under pressure, but not from Ken Bates. It was the pressure of failing in my objective to get the team promoted, and after having such a good season I didn't want it to peter out.' – Simon Grayson*

It wasn't just Millwall who were breathing down Leeds's necks. Swindon Town were just a point behind when they arrived at Elland Road on Easter Saturday, looking to inflict a fourth straight defeat on Grayson's beleaguered team. The final emergency loan window of the season had closed the previous week and with one last throw of the dice Bates sanctioned the addition of yet another winger, Arsenal youngster Sanchez Watt. With Gary McSheffrey written off as a bad job, along with Andy Robinson who was sent on loan to Tranmere, I was hopeful Watt could provide an important option in the final weeks of the season.

It was an emotional occasion at Elland Road as the club marked the tenth anniversary of the deaths of Christopher Loftus and Kevin Speight, two supporters who were murdered in Istanbul on the night before a UEFA Cup semi-final. Richard Naylor and Jonny Howson laid wreaths behind each goal after an impeccably observed minute's silence. Their memories will live on forever.

The mood barely lifted from that point. Leeds started the game outside the top two for the first time all season but should have been buoyed by Millwall being held to a draw the previous day. Instead, it was another lacklustre display, and Leeds were torn apart by a striker who would join them in the summer and assume the nickname 'Barn Door Billy', due to his inability to hit one. Just before half-time Andy Hughes's slip allowed Billy Paynter to convert a simple chance at the far post, and just after the interval Paynter was at it again, turning Hughes, jinking between Kilkenny and Naylor, and unleashing a 20-yard drive that flew into the top corner. It was a stunning goal, although TV replays detected a slight deflection on its way past Higgs. After 55 minutes it was 3-0, with Paynter the provider this time, finding Charlie Austin all alone between Naylor and Collins to nod home from six yards. 'WHAT THE FUCK? WHAT THE FUCK? WHAT THE FUCK IS GOING ON?' asked the Elland Road crowd. I couldn't believe we'd managed to sink to new depths.

What the fuck *was* going on? Leeds were now fourth in the table, level on points with fifth-placed Charlton, and only six points clear of Colchester in seventh. Suddenly it wasn't even inconceivable that they wouldn't make the play-offs. How on earth had it come to this?

Simon Grayson: 'You can be as organised and as fit as you can be, but it's the bit between your ears that's the most important. Every game in League One was tough, and the come-down from the jubilation of Old Trafford was difficult for the players. Plus, the number of fixtures might have caught up with us and we began to lose our way. Then the anxiety and nerves creep in.'

Once back in Harrogate it was time to drink away my sorrows again, and the post-Norwich all-nighter turned out to be a warm-up for a wild Easter weekend. This time the Saturday night after-party was at Burke Street, and after barely a couple of hours of sleep I was on it again on Easter Sunday lunchtime, meeting Lewis, drinking through the day and night, and again ending up back at Burke Street in the small hours for another after-party. Before I knew it, it was Easter Monday lunchtime and Leeds were preparing for kick-off at Yeovil – I'd had only a handful of hours of sleep since the last defeat! Paul, Lewis and I watched the game together just like in the O'Leary years, strangely feeling like a weight had been lifted. Perhaps copious amounts of alcohol and a miserly amount of sleep contributed to the feeling, but I sensed rock-bottom had been hit and this was a fresh start.

It was far from vintage Leeds, but captain Richard Naylor ended the six-hour wait for a goal, and six minutes later he'd scored again. Yeovil pulled a goal back in the second half but a resolute defence held firm during a nervy last 25 minutes, securing a 2-1 victory that ended a run of four defeats. United remained fourth as their rivals won too, but at least Millwall's victory came against seventh-placed Colchester, opening up a nine-point gap that expelled any realistic fears of missing out on the play-offs. But avoiding the play-offs was now the full focus of everybody at the club.

———

Carlisle United 1 Leeds United 3

Matchday 42 of 46
Brunton Park (8,728)

> *'It is very difficult for a team to always be at the same level in a competition as long and competitive as League One. It's normal to hit a pothole, but the important thing is to recover, and we managed it.' – Luciano Becchio*

Leeds returned to Elland Road after the morale-boosting win over Yeovil to entertain Southend United on a bright spring afternoon. Another frustrating occasion was developing as Leeds struggled to break down their stubborn opponents, and on 58 minutes Simon Grayson took the drastic step of substituting the out-of-sorts Jermaine Beckford. Grayson certainly had the Midas touch with substitutions, and once again his change worked a treat. Within two minutes of replacing Beckford with Becchio, the Argentine had won a 50-50 on the halfway line which led to a chance for Max Gradel and the Ivorian beat the keeper at his near post. What a release of tension it was when the Kop net rippled. In the closing stages Gradel turned provider, crossing for Becchio to get on the scoresheet himself, sealing consecutive victories for the first time since December.

With five games remaining the hunted had become the hunters. The pressure was now on Leeds's promotion rivals, and it told for Swindon who slipped up in their first game as holders of the second automatic promotion place. Grayson's men were up to third, and Millwall were the new occupants of the coveted second spot going into the last round of midweek fixtures. The Lions headed to Yeovil, while for Leeds it was a trip to Carlisle, where the Whites had experienced an array of emotions in their four trips during the past three seasons. As Paul and I headed across the A66 we were stunned by the emerging team news – Beckford had been dropped to the bench.

Simon Grayson: 'Regardless of the individual, when you've not been winning games you're looking for a winning formula. We felt as a coaching staff we needed to do something differently, and the decision to drop Jermaine was in the best interests of the team. But we still knew he could play a part, even if it was coming off the bench.'

It's fair to say Beckford had polarised opinion in recent weeks, with some supporters accusing him of showing a lack of commitment to Leeds amid the lure of an imminent move to the Premier League. I suppose it stood to reason; after all, his contract was expiring in a matter of weeks, and if he did pick up a serious injury it wouldn't just cost him a move to the Premier League but potentially his livelihood for a period. That said, Beckford had never been one to be chasing down full-backs, he was an out-and-out striker whose job was to score, but with the goals drying up and his exit on the horizon he became an easy target for the fans.

Jermaine Beckford: 'It was a really difficult time – it genuinely hurt to hear fans speculate like they were. None of it was true, I'd have run through brick walls for the team and the club. Everyone goes through slumps but nobody had seen it with me before.'

Bradley Johnson: 'I've been at clubs where players knew they were leaving and just tossed it off, but that was never the case with Becks, it wasn't in his character. He came in every day and trained to the best of his ability.'

With Gradel alongside Becchio, Leeds lacked none of Beckford's pace and the little Ivorian did the dirty work too as the visitors dominated the first half. Becchio opened the scoring early on, then missed what looked a certain goal to make it 2-0, and Leeds were punished by a former 'O'Leary Baby' when Ian Harte's trademark free kick was headed home by Richard Keogh just before the interval. It was a sickening blow, but the half-time scores provided a nice antidote, with Yeovil leading Millwall 1-0.

Straight after the restart Leeds regained the lead thanks to a clinical Gradel header from Snodgrass's wicked cross, then minutes later Gradel sent Becchio bearing down on goal, and with only Harte chasing him he had all the time in the world to pick his spot and slide the ball under the goalkeeper for 3-1. What a start it had been for Grayson's new strike pairing, and as much as he missed playing with Beckford, Becchio was enthused to have such a high-level alternative to partner him.

Luciano Becchio: 'Max Gradel was a fast player with a lot of quality, who could also understand me very well. Beckford had a brilliant level all year but sometimes it's normal to lower that level a bit. There are so many games.'

The mood on the terracing was buoyant and Beckford was cheered on to the pitch as an 88th-minute substitute. The points were safe by then and all the focus was on Huish Park, where Millwall still trailed 1-0. At the final whistle we celebrated with the victorious Yellows, but as we filed out of the ground the news filtered through that Millwall had grabbed a 93rd-minute equaliser. It was annoying, but it wasn't enough to prevent Leeds from reclaiming that second automatic promotion spot, with just four games now remaining.

—

Leeds United 4 Milton Keynes Dons 1
Matchday 44 of 46
Elland Road (25,964)

> 'How often do you see teams in all divisions have a bit of a wobble? Some get over the line, some don't.' – Simon Grayson

We were coming towards the summer and the first Burke Street barbecue was held on Saturday, 17 April, while listening to Gillingham v Leeds. Millwall had lost 1-0 at Huddersfield on the Friday night, so we lit the coals in the hope that Leeds would win and their other rivals would slip up, thus presenting a chance to seal promotion with a win against MK Dons in the penultimate home game the following week. Unfortunately the rejuvenated Whites reverted to their post-Old Trafford ways, capitulating in front of our ears as the relegation-threatened hosts raced into a 3-0 lead after just half an hour. All three goals were the result of calamitous, late-McAllister set-piece defending, though Becchio did restore some hope when scoring right on half-time.

Both Swindon and Charlton were also losing at the interval, which was clearly a blessing but compounded my annoyance; what a chance we had wasted to take a giant step towards the Championship. I was praying for a miraculous comeback but it wasn't until the 87th minute that the game was truly alive. Substitute Beckford converted from the spot to give hope of at least a point, but no equaliser was forthcoming and we consoled ourselves with the dropped points of Swindon and Charlton. Norwich confirmed their promotion by beating the Addicks, and but for mathematics they would already be champions. It was 'as you were' in the race to join Norwich in the Championship, and second place felt like a poisoned chalice – the team in that position had only won once in seven matches. Everybody seemed to be crawling for the line.

Simon Grayson rang the changes for the visit of MK Dons, who were in disarray with manager Paul Ince not even bothering to turn up for the match, having announced he would be leaving at the end of the season. Howson and Doyle – the midfield pairing for the majority of the campaign – accompanied top scorer Beckford on the bench, Ben Parker returned for his first start since the opening day and 19-year-old Sanchez Watt was handed his full debut, and learned some home truths from Jonny Howson before the game.

> *Bradley Johnson: 'Sanchez Watt, he came from Arsenal and had a red pair of boots. Jonny Howson was like, "You can't wear them." Sanchez didn't understand. "You can't wear red boots, you play for Leeds. You can't wear red, it's Man United."'*

The Kop was in great voice on another sunny afternoon in West Yorkshire, and it was all smiles as Becchio and Gradel continued their sensational form with goals either side of a shock equaliser, from another poorly defended set piece. The architect of the visitors' downfall (not including their AWOL manager) was Watt, whose pace and energy was too much for them to handle. Watt stole the ball off the right-back to set up the opening goal for Becchio, and before half-time it was his sharpness that drew the same defender into a late lunge and a harsh straight red. As the half-time scores were read out the optimism at Elland Road was soaring again; neither Millwall, Swindon nor Charlton were ahead.

Leeds started the second half a goal and a man to the good, and ended it three goals and three men to the good. Beckford moved on to 30 goals for the season by grabbing a brace from the bench, and referee Michael Oliver brandished two more straight red cards, though neither were harsh this time. It was comical seeing 11 vs 8, like watching a training session, but Leeds didn't have enough time to capitalise and build their goal difference, which was looking increasingly likely to be decisive come the end of the season.

At the final whistle the big screen revealed the news that Millwall had ground out a 2-0 victory over Gillingham, but Swindon and Charlton could only draw, leaving them four and five points behind Leeds respectively. It now seemed to be a straight shoot-out between Leeds and Millwall for second place, although the Whites were heading to Charlton for the penultimate game of the season, and defeat would blow the promotion race wide open once again.

———

Charlton Athletic 1 Leeds United 0

Matchday 45 of 46
The Valley (23,198)

> *'I wasn't relying on just getting a point, I wanted to get it over the line as quickly as possible.'* – Simon Grayson

This was a really difficult fixture for Leeds, but that didn't stop us throwing a 'Promotion Party' at Burke Street, just in case. The weather wasn't really good enough for a barbecue but that had never stopped us before; the biggest issue was the streaming of the match. Streaming was a new concept back in those days, and even plugging your laptop into the TV was a phenomenon at the time, but we managed to get the match on the telly and my mates gathered in excited trepidation.

Despite his brace from the bench in the previous game, there was still no place in the starting line-up for Beckford, although Michael Doyle did return to shore up the midfield. At left-back it was all change again after the unfortunate Ben Parker suffered another injury. Shane Lowry returned to the side in his place, left-back number eight of the season, none of whom had appeared in the position more than the ever-willing Andy Hughes.

This would have been an exasperating afternoon at the best of times, but the stream made it even worse. It worked OK initially, but after Gradel wasted an early chance there was constant buffering, making viewing almost impossible. In the end we came to the difficult decision to ditch the stream and listen on the radio, but there was little action to miss as the teams trudged off level at half-time. When they re-emerged they did so with a spring in their step because Tranmere had taken the lead against Millwall. It was good news for Charlton – if they beat Leeds they would go into the final day with a chance of promotion – but for Leeds it was mouthwatering. If they could beat Charlton they were up.

Unsurprisingly the game opened up in the second half, and when news filtered through that Leeds's Andy Robinson had doubled Tranmere's lead against Millwall, the Leeds fans rejoiced and Grayson smelt blood. He wanted to end it right there. There were 25 minutes to go and Grayson introduced Beckford as a third striker – surely he was the best bet to claim the promotion-winning goal. Ten minutes later, Grayson brought on a fourth attacker in Watt, in place of holding midfielder Doyle. It was a bold move, and for once in my life I disagreed with the manager. With a draw Leeds would probably only need one more point for promotion, barring a three-goal Millwall victory on the final day, and it would also close the door on Charlton's promotion bid; one fewer rival to worry about. But Grayson wasn't bothered and ten minutes later he withdrew Andy Hughes, bringing on a fifth forward in Mike Grella.

Simon Grayson: 'With the way the results were going I knew if we won this game we'd be promoted at The Valley. But I also knew it would be in our hands on the final day no matter what, that's why I threw on every forward I could.'

The situation was critical, so we decided to give the stream another go. It worked for long enough to see the ball falling for Beckford in the box, at which point it buffered, leaving the screen frozen and us wondering whether or not we had scored the goal to end our League One nightmare. Incredibly, when the screen finally came back to life it was Charlton who were celebrating, and the score in the corner of the screen confirmed what we could scarcely believe – Charlton had scored an 89th-minute winner. In fact, it was Richard Naylor who scored, and adding to his recent own goal against Gillingham gave rise to a conspiracy theory that claimed our captain was actively trying to scupper his beloved hometown club's promotion bid, sabotaging the goal that he came to Elland Road to achieve, so that he could continue his Whites career in League One the following season.

At full time we were so deflated. We'd been ready to party into the night and had come so close. But thank heavens for Andy Robinson; without him all hope could have been lost. As it was, Leeds had actually achieved their priority for the day – matching Millwall's result guaranteed that a final-day victory against Bristol Rovers would secure promotion to the Championship.

———

Leeds United 2 Bristol Rovers 1

Matchday 46 of 46
Elland Road (38,234)

'It was a game that summed up the last 30, 40 years of Leeds United. All the emotions in one afternoon: the highs, the

lows, the drama, the disappointment, the elation and the relief.' – Simon Grayson

It all came down to this. It was Leeds's 60th game of a season and would go down in the history books, even if they didn't win. They weren't just playing for promotion either, they were also playing for the legacy of the historic victory at Old Trafford, which would be soured forever if Leeds failed to win promotion. This match meant everything.

The situation couldn't be simpler – win and Leeds were up, but if they didn't then things would become a lot more complicated. With Millwall and Swindon just a point behind, both were ready to capitalise if United slipped up. The added complication was that the two closest rivals were playing each other, and if they drew Leeds would still need a point, plus the door would open for Charlton if Leeds lost. And if we're talking slim chances, then Huddersfield Town were also still mathematically in the hunt. If Leeds lost, Millwall and Swindon drew, and Charlton failed to win at Oldham, Huddersfield would snatch promotion with a five-goal victory at Exeter. Amazingly, if seventh-placed Southampton hadn't had ten points deducted, they too would have been in contention, level on points with Huddersfield but with a better goal difference than all the other contenders. Anyway, all this complication made the task clearer. Leeds just had to win.

Bradley Johnson: 'There were nerves in the camp. Going into the last game of the season all we had to do was win to go up, but it's easier said than done. Simon gave us a few days off in the week leading up to the game. He told us just to spend time with our families, recharge, don't think about the game, and then come in on Thursday and we can concentrate on the game.'

Simon Grayson's team sheet brought several surprises. First was the absence of captain Richard Naylor, apparently injured, unless the conspiracy theorists were right all along. Leigh Bromby stepped in alongside Neil Collins at centre-back, with Hughes and Lowry the full-backs. There was no surprise to see Kilkenny and Doyle in midfield, and Grayson recalled Bradley Johnson to the left of midfield, with Max Gradel moved to the right in order to pave the way for the reinstatement of Jermaine Beckford up front with Luciano Becchio, in what would surely be Beckford's last game for Leeds. It was a bold move by Grayson, and bolder still, he made Beckford the captain.

Simon Grayson: 'If somebody's going to enjoy the big stage, go out on a big swansong and leave as a real hero, it's going to be Jermaine, so why not make him captain? We'd had a bit of fun over the season with Becks. Glynn Snodin would sometimes hand him the armband, and when Jermaine took it Snods would say, "Give that to Nayls." So when Snods gave him the armband on this occasion he said, "Yeah, yeah, who am I giving it to today?" But Snods said, "No, you're wearing it!" Becks still thought it was a wind-up until he actually saw it on the team sheet. When he saw he was down as captain he just had this massive smile on his face, "Oh, you're not messing around!"'

Grayson's selection left Leeds with four players on the bench who would be entitled to be annoyed with their manager. Nobody had started more games, appeared more times, or clocked up as many minutes as Jonny Howson and Robert Snodgrass in 2009/10, but after 56 appearances each I suppose they'd earned a little rest. Casper Ankergren had been there from the very start of the League One journey and had starred in the big occasions at Wembley, Old Trafford and White Hart Lane. Ľubomír Michalík had also endured all three

League One campaigns, plus both of these players harboured the experience of being part of the team that brought Leeds to League One in the first place. Wise's team was relegated in spite of Ankergren and Michalík, not because of them, but that must have made them even more determined to help push Leeds over the line.

> *Casper Ankergren: 'It wasn't that I wasn't bothered about not playing, but the most important thing was the club got promoted. I'd had three and a half fantastic years at Leeds and knew I would be leaving in the summer, so to leave them with a promotion would be the perfect end.'*

It was a beautiful summer's day at Elland Road and the players were greeted by a wall of noise as they left the tunnel, in the form of 'Marching On Together'. The fans were belting the song out so loud that I felt a surge of emotion. What passion, what a thing to be a part of. This match meant everything to everyone here. The players must have felt ten feet tall, especially Beckford.

> *Jermaine Beckford: 'Leading Leeds out of the tunnel at Elland Road was incredible. You can hear the rumbling of the stands, the cheering, and as soon as I broke that line from the tunnel to the pitch it was the most incredible sound ever, nothing can touch it. I was walking on the field fighting back the tears, thinking, "Get it together man, you've played here a hundred times!"'*

The match kicked off to a huge roar from Elland Road, which was immediately replaced by a chorus of boos that continued throughout the match whenever the visitors were in possession. The only other teams to receive such treatment in my lifetime were Manchester United and Galatasaray, so the Bristol Rovers players couldn't have experienced anything like this before, nor would they ever again.

Jermaine Beckford: 'The fans made the stadium so hostile. The opposition getting jeered and booed every touch gives you a bit more adrenaline, a little bit more energy to go even harder.'

Leeds sliced the yellow wall open within two minutes of kick-off, but with the goal at his mercy Gradel couldn't get his head on Johnson's cross. A golden chance had gone begging but it was encouraging to have made one so quickly – it was a great start. It was a greater start for Swindon, who took the lead at Millwall and second spot in the live table. News of the goal filtered through the Kop but nobody cared; what was happening on the pitch in front of us was all that mattered, and our team were pumped up and on the top of their game.

On 12 minutes came the next big chance, when Gradel skinned the full-back and rolled the ball across the goalmouth. From the Kop it looked a certain goal, but once again it came to nothing. The noise bellowing around Elland Road was deafening – surely it was a matter of time until Rovers crumbled. On 15 minutes came the news that Millwall had equalised through Steve Morison. Grayson's men were back in second place and attacking again, but with Kilkenny and Beckford waiting for tap-ins, Gradel thrashed at the ball and wasted the chance. By now I was becoming slightly agitated that we weren't ahead, but it was easy to stay positive. Leeds had been first to every ball and won every 50-50, there was absolutely no doubt who wanted it more, and the home fans were revelling in it.

Just as Rovers were about to survive the first half hour, Kilkenny split the defence and Beckford finished into the top corner of the South Stand net. Elland Road erupted, but seconds later came the realisation that the flag was up and the goal wouldn't count; Beckford had been a yard offside. Then suddenly the decibels were raised again as a melee ensued in the South Stand penalty box, with everyone getting involved. The Elland Road crowd love a bit of argy-bargy and belted out a rousing rendition of 'We are Leeds' but nobody in the ground understood the severity of what was happening. We were still oblivious even when the red card was brandished. The reaction of the crowd was to cheer, before the realisation struck again – it was Gradel who had been sent off.

Gradel had already been involved in a few incidents with the visiting left-back, Daniel Jones. He had tackled Jones, skinned him, and just before 'the incident' he had been hacked down by him. When Beckford's goal was disallowed Jones said something and Gradel barged into him in anger, and Jones took his chance to get the winger sent off. The Leeds fans were gobsmacked, and Gradel was apoplectic. It took three Leeds players to drag him away from the referee, but Gradel wouldn't leave the pitch.

Jermaine Beckford: 'I tried to get him off the pitch, but for a little fella he's quite strong! I was trying to reason with him, telling him he was just going to make it worse, but he wasn't hearing it. He was emotionally broken.'

The Leeds fans had had enough, chanting, 'OFF! OFF! OFF!' to their own player. Clearly they were dazed and delirious, as was their manager.

Simon Grayson: 'Like everybody, we were stunned when he got the red card, and stunned that he carried on like he did. Max had lost his head completely. Then all of a sudden it hit home that we've got to win this game with ten men now.'

For the remainder of the half the shell-shocked crowd were mostly silenced, except for the hateful chorus of boos that greeted every touch of Jones, and the cheers when he was fouled or tackled. The fans, like Grayson I'm sure, just wanted to get to half-time, and when half-time came the live table still had Leeds in second place, ahead of Charlton on goal difference, with Swindon and Millwall both a point back and ready to pounce. In my head it was all irrelevant; we were done for.

I sat for the full 15 minutes with my head in my hands, alone with my miserable thoughts, in disbelief at what had happened, contemplating the play-offs and already writing off our chances in that too. What chance would we have after this? The players had been through the mill, and now they were being dragged through a hedge. How could we pull ourselves together and go again after missing out on promotion in such heartbreaking fashion? It would be impossible.

Bradley Johnson: 'I walked into the changing room and just saw these little legs kicking the floor. Max was laid under the bench crying his eyes out, tears of anger. The lads weren't happy, everyone was emotional but Simon came in and sent Max out of the changing room to defuse the situation. Then he told the lads, "We are where we are, whatever has happened just forget about it. I believe we can beat them with ten men and you've got to go out and do that now. We've got 45 minutes to get promoted, our season relies on it." It was a great team talk, but then straight from kick-off...'

Straight from kick-off, disaster truly struck. A deep cross by the villain of the day, Jones, was hooked back across goal and then hooked into the net to the horror of Elland Road. We really were done for.

Ten minutes later, with the crowd still rocked, Grayson made his first substitution of the game, bringing on Jonny

Howson for Shane Lowry, and changing to a 2-4-1-2 formation with Johnson and Hughes down the wings, and Howson supporting the front two. Leeds were going for the jugular. Howson immediately injected impetus, and suddenly the crowd found their voice again. Four minutes later, Johnson slipped as he delivered a cross from deep, screwing the ball low to the edge of the box. Becchio reacted first and laid the ball off for Jonny Howson, who whipped a beautiful 25-yard curler into the top corner at the Kop end. Elland Road exploded. Has he ever scored a better goal? And has he ever scored one better timed? Howson skipped around the pitch, gritting his teeth and waving his arms, communicating to the crowd, 'Come on everyone, we're doing this! We're all in it together and we're going to fucking do it!'

Grayson's Midas touch had come to the fore again, and suddenly there was renewed hope.

Simon Grayson: 'Jonny came on and got the equaliser, and suddenly it was like we were playing with 14 men and they were down to eight or nine. Bristol Rovers had gone mentally; everybody could sense something was going to happen.'

Bradley Johnson: 'When Jonny scored that goal the roof lifted, and Bristol just capitulated. The way the fans reacted made them shit themselves.'

The crowd had barely calmed down when a minute later Leeds were on the attack again. Howson's cross was palmed into the path of Johnson, standing on the corner of the six-yard box with only a defender on the line to obstruct him. Johnson couldn't have struck his shot with more venom, but instead of finding the back of the net he found the back of the Kop, via the tiniest clip off the top of the bar. I couldn't believe it, nobody could, but the ten men's dominance was so encouraging – now we had a game on our hands.

I started to believe it could be done, and the whole of Elland Road was doing everything it could to make it happen. Bristol Rovers were visibly rattled, and in the next passage of play they were caught in possession on the halfway line by Becchio. Leeds steamed forward but the attack was repelled by a sliced clearance straight into the East Stand. The crowd could sense blood, and the most spine-tingling 'Marching On Together' I have ever witnessed boomed around the ground, with the chorus repeating three times at maximum volume. It felt like a force of nature, and when it finished the goalkeeper had collected Becchio's flick-on and attempted a quick throw out to his right-back. However, his attempt was read by Beckford, who jumped and got enough of his head to the ball to divert it into the path of Johnson on the edge of the penalty area. Johnson took it on his chest and powered into the box.

Bradley Johnson: 'My eyes lit up. I looked up at where the keeper was and saw Jermaine was in a better position than me, so I crossed it to Jermaine … Nah, I'm not gonna lie, I did try and shoot, but it was always gonna be Becks that got the winning goal to get us up.'

Johnson's drive flew across the goalmouth, where a lunging defender managed to block it from reaching Becchio. When the ball bounced loose, skipper Beckford was standing where any good striker should be, right in the middle of the bloody goal, and he duly pounced.

Jermaine Beckford: 'Brad took a touch, looked up and saw me, then he took another touch and looked at the goal. I'm thinking, "No! Don't look at the goal!" but he's just leathered it and suddenly it's broke into my path. I had three options:

smash it, lift it over the keeper, or go under him. I made a clean connection, hard and low, and it hit the back of the net. Wow, that was such a moment!'

Leeds had turned it around. The celebrations on the terraces were off the charts; I couldn't believe what was happening and tumbled down the Kop stairs in ecstasy. The Whites had risen from the dead.

As it happens, Millwall had taken a 2-1 lead over Swindon in between the two Leeds goals, meaning four teams had now held the promotion spot at some stage in the afternoon – three different teams in the last three minutes – but the Whites were back in the driving seat and half an hour from promotion. The club anthem echoed around Elland Road. What a noise, what fans, what a club!

Now came the really hard bit, not fucking it up again. I was awash with nerves. The celebrations had carried me from the top of the Kop down around 20 rows, and there I stayed for the rest of the match. I had no idea where Paul was, but I didn't care; in fact, I needed to be alone. I stood with my hands over my mouth for the remainder of the game, only moving to put my hands on my head whenever Bristol Rovers got near the Leeds goal. I'm not even sure I could chant, I was too desperate. Casper Ankergren was suffering similar emotions. He was supposed to be on the bench but the tension was just too much.

Casper Ankergren: 'It was madness, what a game! I was so nervous I couldn't sit still. The groundsmen were watching in a little office, I would go in there, watch on the TV with them, then back out to the bench. It was the longest game of my life!'

If I wasn't chanting then I was the only one, and despite Grayson solidifying the team by changing to a 4-4-1 formation the Whites remained on the front foot, spurred on by their electrified fans. Becchio led the line on his own like a trojan, a battering ram that would not be quelled, and with Howson and Beckford supporting from the wings there was still hope that Leeds could get the third goal to seal the game. There was almost a sting in the tail, but Shane Higgs flew out his goal to dive at the feet of the advancing forward and steal the ball off his toes; 38,000 terrified fanatics sighed with relief.

With 15 minutes remaining more dogged play by Becchio won a free kick in a dangerous position. Kilkenny swung it to the back post and Leigh Bromby rose highest, looping a header back across goal. My heart skipped a beat as Becchio flung himself at the ball, but he couldn't reach it and it cannoned off the post and out to safety. If Bromby's header had been a fraction to the left or a fraction to the right, promotion would have been all but secured.

As we moved into the final ten minutes Leeds became more cautious, happy to sit in two banks of four behind the ball, and happy to play possession football when they had it, amid the anxiously excited din of the home fans in the background. In moments of lower anxiety chants would break out, and during one stint of possession the crowd even mustered the courage to bring out the 'ole' for every Leeds pass. By the time the clock ticked to 85 minutes the nervous tension was palpable, but Grayson's men were doing a fantastic job, with Kilkenny a constant outlet for every one of them, guaranteeing possession would be retained. By now it was unlikely Leeds would lose, so there was some relevance in tracking events at The Den where Swindon had pulled it back to 3-2. If they could score again Leeds would be promoted even with a draw, but that was a get out of jail card nobody wanted to need.

In the 88th minute the fans rose to their feet to salute Becchio, who was substituted to rapturous applause having given every ounce of energy he had. Shortly after, all eyes were on the fourth official. The 90 minutes were up but the amount of added time was not announced; instead, we got an announcement about staying off the pitch (fat chance). Just 90 seconds later the whistles were screeching out from the Leeds fans, desperate to entice the final whistle like in the olden days, but that noise turned to cheers when Sanchez Watt's mazy surge forward was stopped by a cynical foul. By the time this free kick was pumped towards the north-west corner flag, time would surely be up.

It was at this moment that Simon Grayson made his third and final change, match-winner Beckford making way for Robert Snodgrass, to the adulation of the Elland Road crowd. 'JERMAAAAIIIINE BECKFORD, JERMAAAAIIIINE BECKFORD!' There were kisses blown to the crowd before and after Beckford wasted another few seconds by searching out Jonny Howson and sliding the captain's armband on to the youngster himself. It wouldn't have clicked at the time, but this was a poignant moment. The only remaining players from the 2007 pre-season trip to Germany had scored the goals and shared the armband as – three years later – their journey through the abyss was coming to an end. After hugs for his other team-mates there was a final wave to the fans, and Beckford could ride off into the Premier League sunset with his job done and a place in the history books of Leeds United sealed forever. He was leaving as a legend.

With the ball in the corner and four minutes of added time elapsed it felt like job done, and the fans' excitement was about to boil over. It did boil over for some when the referee next blew his whistle, but it wasn't for the end of the game; oddly he had awarded a foul throw. Fans were on the pitch and I was pulling my hair out. 'Why isn't it over? Why the hell was that a foul throw? Where is that bloody PA announcement when you need it? GET OFF THE FUCKING PITCH!' The stewards managed to clear the playing area, and when the ball was eventually hurled down the line the final whistle blew and it was all over. Leeds had done it, promotion was achieved, our League One nightmare was over!

Simon Grayson: 'By the end the officials were just desperate to get off the pitch before the fans came on. The linesman sprinted past me, he'd have beaten Usain Bolt down the tunnel! Seeing grown men kissing the turf, that's how much it meant to everybody, and on the bench it was so emotional, the jubilation, but the relief more than anything.'

As the visitors fled the pitch, the Leeds substitutes, coaches and fans streamed on in delirious celebration, and I went to join them. Paul was now beside me and we headed straight for the huddle of fans who had Andy Hughes on their shoulders, screaming and 'Leeds saluting' at the remaining fans in the Kop. Eventually we made our way to the middle of the pitch and were surrounded by thousands of fans. Strangely the chants weren't our normal promotion offering, to the tune of 'Baby Give It Up'. Instead, it was a 'Three Lions' version that hadn't been sung all season, 'WE'RE GOING UP, WE'RE GOING UP, WE'RE GOING, LEEDS ARE GOING UP!'

The PA announcer was a persistent fellow. 'Please keep off the pitch' was still the message, and eventually we headed back to the Kop to enable our heroes to re-emerge for their lap of honour. When they did come back out the emotion was just too strong and the fans couldn't help themselves from streaming back on to the pitch to pay homage. This was not the vanity invasions that you often see nowadays, this was pure unbridled passion, adrenaline, love and relief. The players were whisked back down the tunnel, and at the second attempt the fans managed to control themselves as Grayson's team embarked upon the lap of honour they had shed blood, sweat and tears for.

Bradley Johnson: 'I remember coming out and jumping and singing, and then I heard this voice on the mic singing "Marching On Together", and it was Max Gradel, and I'm thinking, "You little shit, you almost cost us that game and now you're singing on the mic!" But that was Max, he plays with emotion, and he'd been unbelievable that year for us.'

We finally left the ground, and on the way back into Leeds I checked my phone and had received a text message from my dad, 'Now you know how Nelson Mandela felt!' I couldn't help comparing it to Manchester United's famous 1999 European Cup win, 'the flukiest win in history', and despite the polar opposite glamour, I can't believe their fans felt any different to how we did.

Jermaine Beckford: 'Pure elation and relief, muddled together in a big ball of weirdness! I'd been through so much heartbreak – three play-off defeats and a relegation in four and a half seasons – and after all the hard work, all the frustration, to finally take that humongous step on the road back to where the club deserves to be, was just incredible.'

After a pint in Leeds, we headed back to Harrogate to continue the merriment. We were so elated, it was an incredible feeling, and all we could do was sing and drink. My memories of the night are of course limited (not faded, just limited), but I remember being in Lure Bar and getting the whole place singing, 'NA NA NANA NANA NANA NA NA NA, LEEDS ARE GOING UP, GOING UP, LEEDS ARE GOING UP!' I also remember being in our final destination, Viper Rooms. Paul, Rick and I just couldn't stop chanting. The bouncers were incredibly lenient, to be fair to them, and kept warning us that they'd have to throw us out if we didn't stop, so we would go off and find a quiet corner where we could chant some more, until we were rumbled again and had to find another quiet corner in which to celebrate.

Before the players could properly let themselves go, first they had to attend the end-of-season dinner, ludicrously scheduled for after the last match. As soon as their duties were over the celebrations really commenced. 'You must have been too drained to celebrate, or did you manage it?' I naively asked Johnson.

Bradley Johnson: 'Oh, we managed it! You couldn't not go out, we knew how much it meant to the fans. We all went out together and the city was buzzing, it was an unbelievable night. We celebrated for a few days after that too, then we went to Dubai for a big promotion party. So we celebrated for a good two weeks!'

I would never have thought that the highlight of 18 years as a Leeds United fan would be finishing second in the third tier, but here we were, and it was glorious! It may even have been, or must have been, the most joyous occasion Elland Road had ever seen. From the depths of despair to the most incredible high, it was an emotional roller coaster like no other match I had ever experienced. I can't imagine attending another like it in my life.

I was bouncing off the walls for days afterwards, and the following Friday night I was sat in The Alex on my own, waiting for my mates to arrive, watching Swindon v Charlton in the play-off semi-final. My pint tasted so sweet watching that match, knowing Leeds were already up and taking no part. I was smiling from ear to ear. Then over the speakers played 'Baby Give It Up', and I was overcome by emotion! The overwhelming emotions only arise through the suffering, and my word had we suffered. Finally, it was all over, and the following season we would be gunning for promotion back to where Leeds United truly belong, the Premier League.

Luciano Becchio: 'It was the greatest success I experienced in football. It was fantastic, wonderful. It was also a token of gratitude to all the fans for so much love. It was an unforgettable moment.'

Bradley Johnson: 'I've experienced promotions since, but I've never had a day like Bristol Rovers. I've still got photos up in my house, celebrating Jermaine's goal with a fan in the Kop, and on the fans' shoulders after the game. I still laugh about my reaction to Becks's goal now, jumping up and down, waiting for him to score. I don't think that'll ever get old. Such great memories, I'll never forget that day.'

Jonny Howson: 'I always wanted to achieve something for Leeds. A lot of world-class players have played for the club and not achieved anything, and it didn't matter for me that it was in League One. It could have been League Two, I wasn't bothered. To have that day, and that occasion, the drama of it all, celebrating with all the fans on the pitch, and doing it for your hometown club – how does it get much better than that? It's something I'll look back on for the rest of my life.'

League One Table 2009/10

Norwich City	46	29	8	9	89	47	95
LEEDS UNITED	**46**	**25**	**11**	**10**	**77**	**44**	**86**
Millwall (P)	46	24	13	9	76	44	85
Charlton Athletic	46	23	15	8	71	48	84
Swindon Town	46	22	16	8	73	57	82
Huddersfield Town	46	23	11	12	82	56	80
Southampton*	46	23	14	9	85	47	73
Colchester United	46	20	12	14	64	52	72
Brentford	46	14	20	12	55	52	62
Walsall	46	16	14	16	60	63	62
Bristol Rovers	46	19	5	22	59	70	62
Milton Keynes Dons	46	17	9	20	60	68	60
Brighton & Hove Albion	46	15	14	17	56	60	59
Carlisle United	46	15	13	18	63	66	58
Yeovil Town	46	13	14	19	55	59	53
Oldham Athletic	46	13	13	20	39	57	52
Leyton Orient	46	13	12	21	53	63	51
Exeter City	46	11	18	17	48	60	51
Tranmere Rovers	46	14	9	23	45	72	51
Hartlepool United**	46	14	11	21	59	67	50
Gillingham	46	12	14	20	48	64	50
Wycombe Wanderers	46	10	15	21	56	76	45
Southend United	46	10	13	23	51	72	43
Stockport County	46	5	10	31	35	95	25

*Southampton deducted 10 points
**Hartlepool deducted 3 points

EPILOGUE
The Class of 2010

Shane Higgs
Earnt an extra year on his contract but spent the Championship season as understudy to Kasper Schmeichel before being released. Spent a year at Northampton Town and retired.

Casper Ankergren
Released at the end of the promotion season, signing for Brighton and winning the League One title in 2010/11. Retired in 2017 after Brighton's promotion to the Premier League, although he only made one appearance that season.

Andy Hughes
Signed for Scunthorpe in the 2011 January window, having made ten appearances in the Championship for Leeds. Moved to Charlton in the summer, where he won the League One title in 2011/12 before retiring in 2013.

Jason Crowe
Failed to make a Championship appearance and was released in January 2011. Had short spells at Leyton Orient and Northampton, and retired in 2013.

Ben Parker
Never recovered from his injury problems, making only two Championship appearances for Leeds before he was released in 2012. Spent three years at Guiseley, and two at Harrogate Town, where he retired aged 30 after winning the Conference North play-offs.

Richard Naylor
Remained at Leeds for the 2010/11 Championship season, making 15 appearances. Retired at the end of the following season following 13 Championship appearances for Doncaster, and five for Rotherham in League Two.

Patrick Kisnorbo
Named Leeds' Player of the Year in 2010, but missed the summer's World Cup and the following season due to his Achilles injury. Made 19 Championship appearances in 2011/12 but couldn't recapture his top form. Moved back to Australia in 2013, retiring aged 35 after three seasons with his hometown club, Melbourne City.

Leigh Bromby
Made 23 Championship appearances as backup over the next two seasons, but retired aged 32 after missing the whole of the 2012/13 season through injury.

Ľubomír Michalík
Joined Carlisle for the 2010/11 season and won the Football League Trophy. Moved to Kazakhstan after two more seasons in the Football League, and won the Kazakhstan Cup in 2014. Returned to Slovakia and is still playing at time of writing, aged 38.

Michael Doyle
Received no offer from Leeds and instead joined Sheffield United who were relegated from the Championship. Missed only 13 league games over the next seven seasons, four in League One, and three in League Two, where he won successive promotions in 2017 and 2018 with Portsmouth and Coventry.

Neil Kilkenny
After a successful season in the Championship, Kilkenny was unable to agree new terms and left as a free agent for Bristol

City, and goaded Bates when scoring at Elland Road. Joined Preston two years later and won the League One play-offs in 2015, before ending his career in Australia.

Jonny Howson

Ever present in the 2010/11 Championship season, scoring 11 goals from an advanced role behind Becchio. Appointed club captain for the following season but was sold to Norwich in January 2012 for £2m. After six seasons at Norwich (four in the Premier League), Howson joined Middlesbrough, where he has made over 200 Championship appearances in five seasons.

Bradley Johnson

Missed only one Championship match in 2010/11, playing in a deeper central midfield role. Was unable to agree new terms and joined Norwich as a free agent. Spent three seasons in the Premier League and won the Championship play-offs in 2015 before joining Derby for £6m. Has spent the last six years in the Championship with Derby and Blackburn.

Robert Snodgrass

Excelled in the Championship, but after 13 goals and 14 assists in 2011/12, and being named Player of the Year and taking the club captaincy, Snodgrass was sold to Norwich. Spent nine of the next 11 seasons in the Premier League, which included a £10.2m transfer from Hull to West Ham and ended in relegation with West Brom in 2021. Won 27 caps for Scotland, scoring seven goals.

Max Gradel

Thrived in the Championship, winning the club's Player of the Year award after scoring 18 goals from the wing. Sold on the last day of the 2011 summer window for just £1.7m to Saint-Étienne, where he enjoyed four successful seasons and won the 2013

Coupe de la Ligue. Signed for Bournemouth for £7m but an ACL injury restricted him to 25 Premier League appearances in two years. Regained his top form for Toulouse, and is currently winding down his career in Turkey. Edging towards his 100th cap for Ivory Coast, with 16 goals at time of writing.

Luciano Becchio
Flourished in the Championship, top-scoring with 20 goals. Halfway through the 2012/13 season, with 19 goals already to his name, he was sold to Norwich for £200,000 plus Steve Morison, who had scored one goal in 19 games. Failed to score in 13 Premier League games over the next two seasons, and returned to Argentina's Primera División, where he was plagued by injuries before retiring in Spain.

Jermaine Beckford
Joined Everton on a free transfer and scored eight goals in 34 Premier League games. Spent five of the next six seasons in the Championship for four different clubs, with a loan to Preston in 2014/15 the outlier, where he scored a hat-trick in the League One play-off final to secure promotion. Ended his career at Bury, where injury forced his retirement aged 35. Won six caps for Jamaica, scoring one goal.

Simon Grayson
An excellent run of form saw Leeds second in the Championship at Christmas 2010, but after being denied funds to strengthen a leaky defence the team stuttered, and a run of one win in eight towards the end of the season cost a play-off spot. Halfway through the 2011/12 season, having lost Beckford, Johnson, Kilkenny, Gradel, Kasper Schmeichel and Howson since promotion, and spending less than £2m on transfers, Grayson was sacked with Leeds four points behind the play-off places. Joined Huddersfield and won promotion through the League One play-offs, repeating the trick with Preston in 2015 for his

fourth promotion in four managerial roles. Has failed to taste success since an ill-fated spell at Sunderland in 2017.

Ken Bates

Having dismantled an exciting young squad, Bates spent the proceeds on adding corporate facilities to the East Stand, which reduced the capacity of Elland Road by 4,000 seats and cost the club £7m. With the team stagnating in the Championship, he sold the club to Bahraini shysters GFH Capital in November 2012 for £52m, having bought it for £1.5m from the administrators five years earlier. Bates remained as chairman until the end of the 2012/13 season, by which time the only player remaining from the League One promotion side was Aidy White.

ROLL CALL

	League One 07/08 08/09 09/10			All Comps	Goals
Casper Ankergren	46	35	28	128	0
Shane Higgs	-	-	19	22	0
David Lucas	3	13	-	24	0
Andy Hughes	42	27	38	125	1
Richard Naylor	-	24	28	60	3
Patrick Kisnorbo	-	-	28	34	1
Leigh Bromby	-	-	32	39	1
Jason Crowe	-	-	17	27	2
Ľubomír Michalík	20	19	13	69	1
Aidy White	-	5	8	23	0
Shane Lowry	-	-	10	11	0
Neil Collins	-	-	9	9	0
Rui Marques	37	32	5	82	4
Ben Parker	9	26	4	50	1
Tony Capaldi	-	-	3	5	0
Frazer Richardson	42	23	-	74	1
Alan Sheehan	10	11	-	24	2
Paul Huntington	20	4	-	32	3
Sam Sodje	-	7	-	7	0
Carl Dickinson	-	7	-	7	0
Paul Telfer	-	14	-	18	0

	League One 07/08 08/09 09/10			All Comps	Goals
Mansour Assoumani	-	1	-	1	0
Matt Heath	26	-	-	32	1
Darren Kenton	16	-	-	16	0
Jamie Clapham	13	-	-	15	0
Scott Gardner	1	-	-	2	0
Eddie Lewis	1	-	-	1	0
Jonny Howson	29	43	45	143	15
Neil Kilkenny	19	32	34	104	9
Bradley Johnson	24	17	35	90	10
Robert Snodgrass	-	44	43	107	19
Michael Doyle	-	-	40	50	0
Max Gradel	-	-	31	34	6
David Prutton	46	16	6	78	4
Andy Robinson	-	34	6	50	7
Gary McSheffrey	-	-	9	10	1
Sanchez Watt	-	-	7	7	0
Jonathan Douglas	27	45	-	82	5
Fabian Delph	1	44	-	53	6
Seb Carole	28	-	-	33	3
Ian Westlake	20	-	-	23	3
Alan Thompson	13	-	-	14	3
Curtis Weston	7	-	-	11	1
Peter Sweeney	9	-	-	9	0
Radostin Kishishev	7	-	-	7	0
Filipe da Costa	4	-	-	7	0
Jermaine Beckford	43	36	40	139	85

	League One 07/08 08/09 09/10			All Comps	Goals
Luciano Becchio	-	46	36	101	36
Mike Grella	-	12	16	39	5
Trésor Kandol	43	-	10	61	15
Enoch Showunmi	-	8	7	28	5
Paul Dickov	-	-	4	7	0
Sam Vokes	-	-	8	10	1
Hogan Ephraim	-	-	3	4	1
Lee Trundle	-	10	-	10	1
Liam Dickinson	-	8	-	8	0
Malcolm Christie	-	4	-	5	1
Dougie Freedman	14	-	-	14	6
Marc de Vries	6	-	-	8	1
Tore André Flo	22	-	-	22	3
Anthony Elding	9	-	-	9	1
Leon Constantine	3	-	-	6	2
Wayne Andrews	1	-	-	2	0

AFTERWORD

by Jermaine Beckford

From the first week I was at Leeds United – seeing what the club was all about, the fanbase, the togetherness, the hunger, the ambition – I genuinely wanted to stay there forever, it was amazing! I've scored a hat-trick in the play-off final at Wembley, I've played international football and scored in World Cup qualifiers, but nothing will touch that moment of signing for Leeds. It was the proudest moment of my career and sparked a phenomenal journey that far exceeded my wildest dreams. It was incredible.

My relationship with Leeds United wasn't a love affair, it's a marriage. They helped me to grow as a person and as a footballer, and that's why I have so much admiration for the club and so much to give back. I'm an ambassador for the club now and I still love going in. Even though it's in a different capacity, I still get the same energy, the same emotions, the same feelings when I step out on to the pitch. That will never change, and I know I'm extremely fortunate to have experienced it from a player's perspective. Elland Road is such a special place, it's a conductor for carnage but I found solace in that carnage, it's where I was at my most Zen. I played with a carefree attitude and I loved every minute of it, and I'd like to think I left the fans with those feelings.

What I was able to achieve at such a massive football club, I was proud! I was a young boy who grew up on a council estate who wanted to play football. It didn't matter what level, I just wanted to play football. And I did, for the best team in the world!

WITH THANKS

It was such an honour and a pleasure to speak with the stars of this book, what fine young men! They were so generous with their time, so enthusiastic, and so passionate about Leeds United. They all spoke from the heart, and it was clear to see the respect they still hold for the club and the fans, something that will stay with them forever. Interviewing them was more than a dream come true. A heartfelt thank you to them, and also to the people who put me in touch with those heroes, you have my sincerest gratitude.

Thanks to Jane Camillin for believing in a nobody, and thanks to their fantastic team at Pitch Publishing, who helped make this book such a fine and professional production.

Thanks to my amazing wife, Frankie, for allowing me to spend so much of our free time poring over the many (but never enough) edits. If it wasn't for her I wouldn't be able to curl these things out at a rate of knots.

Thanks to my parents and Gianni for their help and advice, and thanks to Paul for coming to all the games, and Rick for keeping me laughing throughout.

Thanks to my son, Alessandro, for sparking my desire to document my experiences at Elland Road, and last but not least, thanks to Marcelo Bielsa for giving me the experiences worth writing about. The repercussions of his art have infinite recognitions.

Jane Camillin
Pitch Publishing
Frankie
My mum and dad

Gianni Binelli
Paul Male
Richard Ullyett
Casper Ankergren
Simon Grayson
Bradley Johnson
Luciano Becchio
Jermaine Beckford
Jonny Howson
David Prutton
John Crayford
Ben Shires
Miguel Garcia
Nick Gray
Lee Sobot
Leeds That – Leeds United Podcast
James Mooney and Leeds United FC
Kevin Markley: LeedsUnitedMAD
BBC Sport Website
11v11 League Table Generator
Wikipedia
Alessandro Marcelo Dean
Marcelo Bielsa